THE PRINCIPLES OF KINGDOM
FOUNDATIONS

If the foundations are destroyed,
What can the righteous do?
Psalm 11:3

NELSON O. OLAJIDE

authorHOUSE®

AuthorHouse™
1663 Liberty Drive
Bloomington, IN 47403
www.authorhouse.com
Phone: 1-800-839-8640

Published by AuthorHouse   11/15/2012

ISBN: 978-1-4772-4599-6 (sc)
ISBN: 978-1-4772-4600-9 (e)

CONTENTS

DEDICATION—(i)

THIS BOOK IS dedicated to My Saviour, The Champion of my Faith, The King of Kings and Lord of Lords, The **Lord Jesus Christ,** The Captain of my Salvation and the Ultimate Foundation of my life.

It is also affectionately dedicated to my wife, my best friend and helpmate of many years, **Mary Oluwakemi Olajide** whose personal ministry, love, care, encouragement, support and prayers has helped me more than words can convey, not only before but also during and hopefully long after the writing of this book, also to my dearly beloved children and joy of my life, **Rachael Temitope** and **Stephen Olanrewaju (Jnr.)**

ACKNOWLEDGEMENT—(ii)

A BIG THANK YOU goes to my mentor and Spiritual father, Dr. (Rev) N. D. Osameyan, Africa Area Director, World Thrust International, South Africa and his wife Rev. M. Osameyan for their constant support through prayers and encouragement

Great appreciation also goes to Reverend (Dr.) David Owen, Elim Pentecostal church, U.K, for the proof reading, valuable suggestions and observations. Thanks a lot.

Also thanks to my dear friend and brother in Christ, Rev. Nic Burn for his support with the book, thanks a lot, I pray that God will continue to bless you abundantly.

FOREWORD—(iii)

$\mathbf{W}$E ALL APPRECIATE the beautiful buildings scattered all over our cities and towns but only few of us consider the quality of foundations that support them until there is a threat of collapse. My experience in Construction industry clearly shows me that the stability of the superstructure we see depends mostly on the substructure or foundation that is often invisible.

Rev. Nelson Olajide has successfully explored the importance of foundation in all areas of our life's endeavour using the contemporary physical structure to illustrate and emphasize the spiritual dimension of building our lives, marriages, businesses, doctrine and ministry on the Rock that is Christ Jesus

(Isa. 28:16).

The Principle of Kingdom Foundation helps us gain an understanding of the fact that the stability of a building against weather, rain, wind and earth movement depends on its foundation just as the success of all our life's endeavours depend on what we are building upon either faulty, fake, false or good foundation. It also provides an insightful thought on the parable of the wise and foolish builders who both expended their efforts in terms of time, treasure and energy but because the foolish builder was looking for easy way out, he built his house upon the sand. His own house could not stand the test of time, it fell when the heavy rain and storm came on it

(Matt.7: 24-29).

The author in a brilliant biblical investigation also compared and contrast lives of some Bible characters like King Saul and King David, Ithamar and Eli whose foundations were later corrupted resulting in the destruction of their kingdom and priestly ministry.

He charged every reader to re-examine his or her foundation so as to be able to stand the test, trial, temptation, suffering and storms of life.

With a great sense of balance, Rev. Olajide courageously proffers some biblical remedies for rectifying faulty life's foundations.

Since questions help us bring to the surface what is most important, this book does just that by repeating the old question.

"If the foundations are destroyed, what can the righteous do?"
(Psalm 11:3).

The author whom I know very well as a consistent servant of God and had been privileged to mentor over three decade ago has offered some spiritual insights for dealing with the challenge of building on and sustaining a solid foundation for our lives that I recommend you to consider.

Nicholas D. Osameyan Dr. Min, Dr. Di.
Africa Area Director
World Thrust International

PREFACE—(iv)

THE FOUNDATION WE choose to build upon is the source of our success or failures in life. No marriage succeeds nor business lasts without a solid foundation, equally, no country triumphs or ministry experiences breakthrough without one being laid well. They are connected to every aspect of our lives, many of us have seen family' growing or breaking up as a direct result of the foundations they have built upon. Beloved, the purpose of this book not only reveals the effects of a wrong foundation, but, offers a remedy for such a bad foundation

"If the foundations are destroyed, what can the righteous do?" (Psalm 11:3 KJV)

The purpose of identifying and establishing what foundation a person is really building their life upon, ultimately reveals the enigma that so easily shrouds each of us in mystery as to who we really are! The requirement facing each of us is simple; we are all in the process of answering what appears to be the riddle of life, yet this is simply solved by the way we choose to live out our life, however, none of us can 'live out our life' or exist, without first deciding upon which foundation we are going to build our life upon, and, having made that decision, then embarking upon the process of building is straightforward.

We each individually will answer for the choice of foundation we have personally chosen to build upon when we ultimately give an account for our choice of foundation! Without requiring an answer at this stage, can I pose a question for you to consider? Could you tell me, at this stage of your life, what foundation you have chosen to build your life upon? Do you know you have chosen the right foundation? And, if you now believe you have made a mistake and chosen the wrong foundation, can you now change your mind and start using a different foundation?

This book is designed to enable you to answer these questions.

As you read, ask yourself sincerely regarding the problems you have experienced and the ones you are facing right now. Ask yourself; Are the foundations of my marriage; business; Career; Education and Spiritual life, are they the right choice?

If not, the obvious question to ask is: Why Not? My prayer for you my friend is that you may find the answer you seek, that you may discover joy; peace; victory and fulfilment as you discover the good foundation upon which to build, if you choose the right foundation upon which to build your life, it will stand firm when the storms come by laying the right foundation for YOUR LIFE.

CHAPTER—1

Defining Foundation

THE BASIS OR groundwork of anything; the moral starting point for both society and religion; the natural or prepared ground or base on which a structure rests; the lowest division of a building, wall, bridge etc., usually of either masonry; rock; concrete or clay, and, partly or wholly below the surface of the ground is the foundation of the structure. Laying a foundation is; 'the act of founding, setting up, establishing something or the base upon which something stands.

The foundation once laid can be referred to as the origin or root from which growth or building work begins, the starting point, the base upon which all above is built, the point of commencement, thus the beginning of everything has a foundation from which it grew. Everything that has a beginning has, therefore, a foundation upon which it was established, even and including the world in which we live.

The Scripture says: *"In the beginning God created the heavens and the earth. And the earth was without form and void;*

and darkness upon the face of the deep. And the spirit of God moved upon the face of the waters." (Genesis 1; 1&2)

The Holy Bible clearly declares God as the creator of both the universe and this entire world. Since God is the creator, the world was made godly and everything He created was also godly until the ungodly attitude was introduced into the godly world and thereby polluted and infected His creation and thereby undermined the foundation upon which man had started to build. God, as put forward in the Holy Bible, was both the creator and provider for Adam and Eve, until the devil infected the holy relationship with a deadly virus called sin.

Ever since sin entered into man and creation, the foundational relationship set up by God for man, which man had started to build his life upon, changed, the changes manifested in many ways, including cultural and religious ideology. The foundation of God and man in harmonious fellowship had been undermined, the sinful infection caused a destructive breakdown in this special relationship between man and his maker, thus, man, began to establish his own foundation of beliefs and opinions upon which he would now build.

In Matthew chapter 7 and verse 24 in the Message Bible Jesus said; *"These words I speak to you are not incidental additions to your life, homeowner improvements to your standard of living. They are foundational words, words to build a life on. If* you work these words into your life, you are like a smart carpenter who built his house on solid rock.

If you read Matthew chapter 7, verses 24 to 27 in the New King James Version, it reads as follows: *24 "Therefore whoever hears these sayings of Mine, and does them, I will liken him to a wise man who built his house on the rock: 25 and the rain descended, the floods came, and the winds blew and beat on that house; and it did not fall, for it was founded on the rock. 26 But everyone who hears these sayings of Mine, and does not do them, will be like a foolish man who built his house on the sand: 27 and the rain descended, the floods came, and the winds blew and beat on that house; and it fell. And great was its fall."*

The foundation of every building not only determines its lifespan but also its security and durability. The size of a building must correspond to the foundation that has been laid, the bigger the building the stronger the foundation. A wise construction engineer spends more time and resources on the foundation of a building than any other part of the building. Every foundation is structured to carry a specific type of building in specific geographical or demographical locations.

For example, due to the frequent earthquakes in Japan, the Japanese government invested billions of dollars on research and have developed many types of foundations, such as flexible foundations. Many of their newly constructed skyscrapers have a special foundation, these are laid using the seismic vulnerability method, naturally, anti-earthquake buildings in Japan are designed to prevent the building from collapse during an earthquake.

This technological innovation is to enhance the stability of the building against possible earthquake damage, that instead of the common rigid type of foundation we are used to, the new elastically made foundation under the seismic method allows the building to move or bend but not give way during the vibration of an earthquake and thus have minimal effect on the structure and enhance human safety.

If it takes such a great sacrifice of financial investment, materials and mental effort to construct a foundation capable of withstanding an earthquake, then this demonstrates the principles of Jesus as outlined above, stressing the importance of laying a good foundation cannot be over emphasized.

CHAPTER—2

Laying A Right Foundation

WHENEVER A GOOD foundation is being laid, it is not laid with the present situation in mind, but in anticipation of future consequences, remember Jesus word on laying a good foundation, He relates to your life and points out that you should be like a 'smart carpenter' who built his house on solid rock. The question then asks: What is the solid rock He is referring to that you should build your life on?

In Matthew chapter 7 and verses 21 to 27 in the Amplified bible we read the following:

²¹ Not everyone who says to Me, Lord, Lord, will enter the kingdom of heaven, but he who does the will of My Father Who is in heaven. ²² Many will say to Me on that day, Lord, Lord, have we not prophesied in Your name and driven out demons in Your name and done many mighty works in Your name? ²³ And then I will say to them openly (publicly), I never knew you; depart from Me, you who act wickedly [disregarding My commands]. ²⁴ So everyone who hears these words of Mine and acts upon them [obeying them] will be like a sensible (prudent, practical, wise) man who built his house upon the rock. ²⁵ And the rain fell and the floods came and the winds blew and beat against that house; yet it did not fall, because it had been founded on the rock. ²⁶ And everyone who hears these words of Mine and does not do them will be like a stupid (foolish) man who built his house upon the sand. ²⁷ And the rain fell and the floods came and the winds blew and beat against that house, and it fell —and great and complete was the fall of it.

Everyone, that includes Me, it also includes YOU! Jesus says; whosoever hears, that is hears His teaching in Matthew Chapter 5,6 and 7, and having heard what Jesus has taught, then goes out and obeys His teaching.

They go and implement the doctrine of Jesus, he who does them, acts out in their life what Jesus has taught, they are called wise by Jesus, He says, in obeying His teaching this action means they are building their life upon rock, by obeying His teaching and living by it, we are likened to one who builds their life on a foundation of rock, which is doing what Jesus Christ teaches. Could the wise man be equalled to a person who sacrifices his present way of living, how they want and live now and instead, live how Jesus teaches they should live doing what He teaches is what we should do? Could that person be likened to one who lives wisely now knowing they will receive in the future amazing benefit!

Would you consider Esau foolish to have sold his birth right for a bowl of delicious stew to satisfy his present intense hunger? So many Christians today seem to exchange their spiritual birth right by focusing their attention on their present need and provide for them at all cost. Is that a foolish thing to do according to Jesus?

Those who hear every single word, every single saying of Christ, they know them, can quote them, even tell you where they are in the new Testament, however, they fail to implement them, they may not realise, but they are sitting down midway to heaven, and that will never bring them to their journey's end. Jesus as both teacher and Lord, gave his own authoritative sayings and commands and expects obedience.

The practical implementation of Christ's teaching is being hampered by believers who are often unconscious of the degree to which their thinking has been shaped and influenced by the world's thinking, rather than by 'The Gospel of Jesus Christ'. For Christ's glory to be manifested in our lives, all else must give way to *Christ's teaching!* Obedience to His teaching is the principal key to success in every area of our lives.

Unfortunately, many people have engaged themselves in twisting Christ's words and calling it a ministry, twisting the word of the Lord to suit their purpose or belief. Sometimes, it might be amusing how unbelievers, otherwise having little or no interest in Scripture, will try to justify the act of severe retaliation by quoting the Old Covenant "eye for eye, tooth for tooth" principle. Sadly, professing believers often hide behind the same defence to vindicate retaliatory actions. The teaching that has its starting point with the example and teaching of Christ, however, simply does not permit us to "render evil for evil." On the contrary, we are specifically instructed:

38 Ye have heard that it hath been said, An eye for an eye, and a tooth for a tooth: 39 But I say unto you, That ye resist not evil: but whosoever shall smite thee on thy right cheek, turn to him *the other also. **40** And if any man will sue thee at the law, and take away thy coat, let him have thy cloke also. **41** And whosoever shall compel thee to go a mile, go with him twain. **42** Give to him that asketh thee, and from him that would borrow of thee turn not thou away.*

(Matthew Ch5v38-42 AV)

Interesting to note, the Apostle Paul and the Apostle John both taught what Jesus taught, in the following verses the same teaching clearly in presented in other parts of the New Testament.

"If it is possible, as much as depends on you, live peaceably with all men. [19] Beloved, do not avenge yourselves, but rather give place to wrath; for it is written, "Vengeance is Mine, I will repay, says the Lord. [20] Therefore if your enemy is hungry, feed him; If he is thirsty, give him a drink; For in so doing you will heap coals of fire on his head. [21] Do not be overcome by evil, but overcome evil with good."

(Romans 12:18-21)

Mary, the mother of Jesus preached one of the greatest sermons at the wedding in Cana of Galilee "as she said to the servants, "*Whatever He says to you, do it.*" (John 2:5) This is a call to submissively obey Christ's command without subtraction, omission, alteration and addition.

Jesus teaches as one example in Matthew 5:43 Jesus teaches that instead of following the teaching of Moses that says;

"You shall love your neighbour and hate your enemies"
(Deuteronomy 23:3-6),

Jesus goes on to say; "But *I say to you, love your enemies bless those who curse you, do good to those who hate you and pray for those who despitefully use you and persecute you . . .*"

(Matthew 5:44-48)

Our heavenly father is the reference point for this way of life (Matthew 5:48). He has shown goodness and mercy even to the ungrateful and wicked (Matthew 5:45; Luke 6:35). We would only be able to stop loving those who are lovable, lending only to those who are reliable, giving only to those who are grateful and recognizing only those who are noble the moment we grasp and are grasped by the unconditionality of the goodness of God. (Luke 6:35-36)

Therefore, whosoever hears the teachings of Jesus and does not obey or implement them, regardless of their religious status, titles or numbers of miracles they have performed and demons they may have cast out, regardless of the sick that have been healed (remembering, all the healings proceed from God. (Exodus 15:26), if you disregard and disobey the teachings of Jesus, you are, according to the doctrine laid down by Jesus Christ Himself, 'YOU ARE' the foolish man who is building on the sand.

There is good news; it is not too late for you or I to revisit our foundation, we need to be sincere before God, change from the sand to the Rock by repenting and then obeying and implement the teachings of Christ so as to be assured that we will not end up facing Jesus and hear Him say, "depart from me" (Luke 13:27).

A good builder thinks less of the building to start with, and focuses on the foundation that will carry the weight of the building they are going to build.

The question now is why must we build on a strong foundation? Everybody **involved in,** laying a foundation in the **physical realm** should be mindful of the future that awaits them, the location of your building determines the type of foundation to be constructed, for example, building on swampy area is different from building on the mountain, building on places where there is constant natural disasters like earthquake, Hurricane, Tornado etc. is different from the one built in disaster free areas, above all, life is full of surprises and challenges becomes inevitable as we aspire for a successful future.

Life's dreams are shattered, marriages crumbles, business fold up, because of the defective foundations, Jesus **says** in Matthew 7 verse 25 "and the rain descended, the floods came, and the winds blew and beat on that house; and it did not fall, for it was founded on the rock."

Note in His word, *". . . and the rain descended . . ."* does not suggest the probability of rain and flood and storms but certainty. Storms in life are inevitable. They will happen. The type and the forms may be different. You will certainly experience them, Jesus said in John 16:33 "These things I have spoken to you, that in Me you may have peace. In the world you will have **tribulation**; but be of good cheer, I have overcome the world".

If you're not in a storm right now, you most probably might have just passed through one or you are about to enter, Storms are part of life. In James 1:2 it says "Count it all joy when you fall into various trials . . ." It does not say *"If you fall into trials."* He did not say might, in other words, what the Lord seems to be saying is that trial is the passage way to glory.

In Matthew 8:23-27 *"²³ Now when He got into a boat, His disciples followed Him. ²⁴ And suddenly a great tempest arose on the sea, so that the boat was covered with the waves. But He was asleep. [25] Then His disciples came to Him and awoke Him, saying, "Lord, save us! We are perishing!"[26] But He said to them, "Why are you fearful, O you of little faith?" Then He arose and rebuked the winds and the sea, and there was a great calm. [27] So the men marveled, saying, "Who can this be, that even the winds and the sea obey Him?"*

Storms are unpredictable. They are sudden and come unexpectedly. The magnitudes of the storms are unpredictable. In this passage, the Bible says, "Suddenly, (Without warning) a furious storm came up "No matter how much we try, we cannot predict the things that will happen to us. The fate of the future is not in our hands but in the hand of the One who holds the keys to our lives. Storms are unpredictable, what we can do is to prepare for it.

The impartiality of the storms: Everybody experience stormy period in one time or the other in our lives. There is clear difference between experiencing storms and affected by storm

Being a Christian does not exempt us from experiencing stormy period. I will like to correct the notion that only bad or disobedient people experience storms. That is very untrue. Remember that the disciples got into a storm in the first place because they obeyed God. Jesus said, *"Get in the boat."* They got in the boat and they sailed right into a storm.

The disciple's, by sailing into the storm were obeying God. They were in the centre of His will. And they were right in the middle of a storm. On the same day, when evening had come, He said to them, *"Let us cross over to the other side." 36 Now when they had left the multitude, they took Him along in the boat as He was. And other little boats were also with Him. 37 And a great windstorm arose, and the waves beat into the boat, so that it was already filling . . ."* That is to say that the boat is full of water, normally, when a boat is full of water it sinks, but why is the Lord's boat filled and still floating?

Because of the presence of Jesus in the boat! When Jesus is in the boat of your life, even though your boat is filled with water of challenges, sickness or every kind of tribulations, it will never sink, because, the Saviour is on board. His presence keeps afloat every boat we found ourselves in.

Is Jesus Christ on board of the boat of your life today? If not, invite Him into your life today and you will not have to worry about any storm anymore, even though it comes, you can be rest assured of absolute safety in the midst of storms.

(Mark 4:35-37

When you're going through a tough time, don't automatically assume,

"I must have been out of the will of God."

Though this may often times lead to it but you might also be at the centre of His will and still experience storms.

Elijah was at the very centre of God's will yet he experienced storms of famine though not affected by it. (1 King17: 7-8).

Storms are not generally an indication of your sinfulness but a revelation of the state and type of foundation you are built on.

The duration of the storm:

Storms only last for few minutes or an hour, but the aftermath leaves a great destruction that could take years or the whole lifetime to rebuild. Tsunami, Fukushima and Hurricane Katrina are just few examples of the destruction a storm can cause, only solid foundation brings peace, security and protection during the storm. Storms therefore are designed to serve as check and balance to your foundation.

The fact is, God has not promised us a storm-free life. Jesus said, "*These things I have spoken unto you, that in Me ye might have peace. In the world ye shall have tribulation, but be of good cheer: I have overcome the world.*"

(John 16:33)

There are two ways we can respond to storms. The way the disciples responded and in the way that Jesus responded. One responded in fear, one responded in faith. One trembled, the other trusted **(Jesus did not doubt God's Word)**

Consequently, in constructing our life's foundation, it is important to be mindful of possible Test and Temptation awaiting us.

To withstand the TESTING DAY, Jesus did not say that if the wind, the flood or storm comes, He said ". . . And the rain fell and the floods came and the winds blew and beat against that house, your foundations has to be laid with rain, floods and wind in mind and it did not fall, because they had dug down to the foundation and built upon the foundation: our job is to discover the foundation, then, once you discover the foundation already laid by God, we then build upon it, thus the house we build will stand

CHAPTER—3

Place Of Trials In Building A Right Foundation

Our HEAVENLY FATHER has designed us for progress, but progress hardly comes without a test, as test often comes before the testimony, There is nobody that God ever used in the Bible that has not gone through the baptism of trials, from our patriarch Abraham (Genesis 15:2; 16:1-2;22:1-14, Isaac (Genesis 26:15-22); Jacob (Genesis 37:33); Joseph (Genesis 33:27,39:1-20); Moses (Exodus 2:11-15), Naomi and Ruth (Ruth 1:1-5), Hannah (1 Samuel 1:2-10), David (1 Samuel 18:10-15,19:8-10, 2 Samuel 15:13-23), Elijah (1 King 19:1-4(, Job (Job1:13-21), Daniel (Daniel 6:16-24), Shadrach, Meshach and Abednego (Daniel 3:13-25) the list is endless, above all and most importantly, our Lord and Saviour, Jesus Christ. ". . . And He himself was tested but yet without sin (Hebrew 4:15) KJV

To follow Christ is to "walk as Jesus did" (1 John 2:26). He did not enter into his resurrected glory until he had first emptied the cup of suffering his Father had given him to drink, he demonstrated absolute submission and perfect obedience through suffering

(Matt.26: 39-42; Luke24: 26, 46; John7: 39, 18:11, 1Pet. 1:11)

So as you can see ". . . Now that we know what we have Jesus, this great High Priest with ready access to God let's not let it slip through our fingers. We don't have a priest who is out of touch with our reality. He's been through weakness and testing, experienced it all but the sin. He knew no sin by personal experience
(John8: 46; Heb.7: 26; 1Pet2: 22; 1John 3:5.

To know no sin is to be free from sin. He says, then, that Christ, while he was entirely exempt from sin, was made sin for us.

The innocent was punished voluntarily as if guilty, that the guilty might be gratuitously rewarded as if innocent "who Himself bore our sins in His own body on the tree, that we, having died to sins, might live for righteousness — by whose stripes you were healed.

(1 Peter 2:4).

"Such are we in the sight of God the Father, as is the very Son of God himself let us walk right up to him and get what he is so ready to give. Take the mercy and accept the help.

(Hebrews 4:14-16) MSG

There is no way we can understand the real concept of Foundation without understanding the Importance of Christian trials; *"Blessed is the man that endureth temptation: for when he is tried, he shall receive the crown of life, which the Lord hath promised to them that love him. Let no man say when he is tempted, I am tempted of God: for God cannot be tempted with evil, neither tempteth he any man"*

(James 1:12-13)

Though, we erroneously use the word trial and temptation as if they are of the same meaning, but there is clear difference between them.

Temptation is an enticement or allurement to do something often regarded as unwise, wrong, or immoral, an attraction or strong appeal to commit immorality.

Trial on the other hand is a tentative or experimental action in order to ascertain results, trial is a test; it is an examination to test your knowledge, ability, Faith or loyalty.

What differentiates the trial from the temptation is the intention behind it. For example, the intention of an examiner, weather in institutions of learning or working places is to test the ability of adaptation, comprehension or capability.

The examiner of a particular student looks with the motive of moving the students to the next level educationally or by your status. No good examiner while examining the students, tempts them by exposing the answer sheets and latter punish them for cheating. That will no longer be regarded as an examiner but a tempter.

The Devil really tried to entice, allure and attract the Lord with the things of this world, as he said to Him; look around, I will give all to you.

"Then was Jesus led up of the Spirit into the wilderness to be tempted of the devil. And when he had fasted forty days and forty nights, he was afterward an hungered. And when the tempter came to him, he said, "If thou be the Son of God, command that these stones be made bread". But he answered and said, "It is written, Man shall not live by bread alone, but by every word that proceedeth out of the mouth of God".

Then the devil taketh him up into the holy city, and setteth him on a pinnacle of the temple, And saith unto him, "If thou be the Son of God, cast thyself down: for it is written, He shall give his angels charge concerning thee: and in their hands they shall bear thee up, lest at any time thou dash thy foot against a stone". Jesus said unto him, "It is written again, Thou shalt not tempt the Lord thy God."

Again, the devil taketh him up into an exceeding high mountain, and sheweth him all the kingdoms of the world, and the glory of them; And saith unto him, "All these things will I give thee, if thou wilt fall down and worship me." Then saith Jesus unto him, "Get thee hence, Satan: for it is written, Thou shalt worship the Lord thy God, and him only shalt thou serve." Then the devil leaveth him, and, behold, angels came and ministered unto him.

(Matthew 4:1-11)

A lot of Christians with weak, shaky and unbalanced foundations have sold their birthright and their God given glory for the passing pleasures of this world, or, compromising their faith applying doctrines of man over the doctrine of Christ.

The Devil also has a purpose, which is, to kill, steal and destroy.

"The thief cometh not, but for to steal, and to kill, and to destroy: I am come that they might have life, and that they might have it more abundantly."

(John 10:10)

As mentioned above, Trial is a tentative or experimental action in order to ascertain results, trial is a test; it is an examination to test your knowledge, ability, Faith or loyalty and to see how and if you apply what you profess.

All through the Bible, there are tested and proven believers, people who are tested by God Himself, or whom He allowed to be tried; there is none of His servants who are immune to trials.

Starting from Adam, Adam was not tempted; Eve was tempted by the devil (Serpent) but God allowed Adam to be tried.

"The LORD tests the righteous, but the wicked and the one who loves violence His soul hates".

(Psalm 11:5)

"For Adam was first formed, then Eve. And Adam was not deceived, but the woman being deceived was in the transgression.

(I Timothy 2. 13&14)

It was God Himself, who tested our patriarch Abraham:

"And it came to pass after these things that God did tempt Abraham, and said unto him, Abraham: and he said, Behold, here I am. 2. And he said, Take now thy son, thine only son Isaac, whom thou lovest, and get thee into the land of Moriah; and offer him there for a burnt offering upon one of the mountains which I will tell thee of"

(Genesis 22:1&2)

God tested Abraham with the intention to promote him eternally; the purpose of the test is to know whether he fears Him and that he willingly surrenders all that he has unto God even the most treasured thing in his life.

Abram believed that there is nothing he has that has not been given to him and there is nothing he gave that he has not received, we can ask ourselves this question, what is it that we have that we have not received and what is it that we were asked to give that has not been giving to us?

Abraham is a good steward of God's resources, what of you?

"And the angel of the LORD called unto him out of heaven, and said, Abraham, Abraham: and he said, here am I. And he said, Lay not thine hand upon the lad, neither do thou anything unto him: for now I know that thou fearest God, seeing thou hast not withheld thy son, thine only son from me.

(Genesis 22:15)

God took the children of Israel through the wilderness for 40 years to try them, and it is very clear that their foundation of faith affected their relationship with God and their testimonies.

"All the commandments which I command thee this day shall ye observe to do, that ye may live, and multiply, and go in and possess the land which the LORD sware unto your fathers. And thou shall remember all the way which the LORD thy God led thee these forty years in the wilderness, to humble thee, and to prove thee, to know what was in thine heart, whether thou wouldest keep his commandments, or no"

(Deuteronomy 8:1&2)

The case of Job is another case of being tried by God and tested by the Devil.

"Now there was a day when the sons of God came to present themselves before the LORD, and Satan came also among them. And the LORD said unto Satan, Whence comest thou? Then Satan answered the LORD, and said, from going to and fro in the earth, and from walking up and down in it. And the LORD said unto Satan, Hast thou considered my servant Job, that there is none like him in the earth, a perfect and an upright man, one that feareth God, and escheweth evil?

Then Satan answered the LORD, and said, Doth Job fear God for nought? Hast not thou made an hedge about him, and about his house, and about all that he hath on every side? Thou hast blessed the work of his hands, and his substance is increased in the land. But put forth thine hand now, and touch all that he hath, and he will curse thee to thy face. And the LORD said unto Satan, Behold, all that he hath is in thy power; only upon himself put not forth thine hand. So Satan went forth from the presence of the LORD.

(Job 1:6-12)

The solid spiritual foundation of Job determines the outcome of his trial. Job's spiritual life was built on the solid foundation, how about yours? Read what the Bible says of Job *"There was a man in the land of Uz, whose name was Job; and that man was perfect and upright, and one that feared God, and eschewed evil"*

(Job 1:1)

CHAPTER—4

Place Of Vision In Building A Solid Foundation

Back to the parable of Jesus Christ in Matthew 7:24-27 *"Therefore whoever hears these sayings of Mine, and does them, I will liken him to a wise man who built his house on the rock: 25 and the rain descended, the floods came, and the winds blew and beat on that house; and it did not fall, for it was founded on the rock. 26 but everyone who hears these sayings of Mine, and does not do them, will be like a foolish man who built his house on the sand: 27 and the rain descended, the floods came, and the winds blew and beat on that house; and it fell. And great was its fall."*

Both wise and foolish men had the same opportunity, both could claim to start out listening to what Jesus said, however, they had a different vision, one was to achieve the goal by doing what Jesus said, living a life of obedience to His teachings, the other was to hear what Jesus taught, then think about what He said, learn about it, know what He said, but live a life the way they knew best, the way they saw others live, others who profess to be following Jesus, live how those they respected said live, live how they knew others would notice, would respect, however, fail to live according to how Jesus said they were to live.

First, let us consider what 'Vision' in the context of living is; 'Vision' is the act or power of living whilst anticipating that which will or may come to pass.

Note first of all the comparisons between these two men in our text; Jesus described two builders constructing houses. One builder, according to Jesus was wise; the other, however, was foolish, one built to gratify the present needs and the other built not just for the present need but also in anticipation of the future challenges.

Building not just for shelter but also for security, not just because of the materials they had at hand and so used these with ease, but because of how and where the foundation was to be laid, went to the effort of digging down and laying the foundation that the master builder had specified.

The fundamental difference between the two foundations is this: One builder patiently endured the pain, the time, the cost and the difficulty of living a life of obedience, as if he was digging and working, breaking the stones and taking care to read and follow the instructions so as to be able to lay his foundation on the rock, while the other ignored the fundamental rules of construction as laid down by the master builder, which they knew, having been given a copy, yet they decided to take shortcuts, which was probably much faster, a lot easier and at a much reduced cost to himself, he ended up building his house on sand.

These two builders probably built structurally similar houses, in other words, they appeared to look the same from the outside, in fact, anyone passing by may well believe they were built by the same builder, because they looked so similar; perhaps they even build in the same area, even in the same street. Thus the same storm ended up battering both houses. However, the houses were different, the foundation each was built upon made a lot of difference between one house standing and the other falling. That was the essential factor for their ultimate security; the foundation we use for our personal life is the essential factor for our welfare.

Another way of looking at this: Jesus gives us the gift of righteousness, we don't earn it, we receive it as a gift when we repent of our way of living, which will result in death, we turn our back on our way of living and thank Jesus for his blood being shed on The Cross, which, if we repent and accept He died in our place so we can be forgiven,

We are forgiven when we recognise and accept why He died. We get the gift of eternal life; we keep it by continuing to trust in Him. At the outset we are given clean garments of righteousness, these are given so we now can approach our Father confidently, in faith, through Christ's finished work on The Cross. So what is our task? Simply put, our task is to keep the garments, which we have been given as a free gift, the garments of righteousness 'CLEAN'!

We are to recognise what we have been given, accept them with thanksgiving, wear them with humility and respect, working to keep them clean. Our life style will either soil them or keep them clean. So how we live is very important. If we do defile them in any way, our job is to swiftly act, repent and have them cleansed. Grace is commonly referred to as 'unmerited favour', and so it is. The favour of God is given to each one of His children, who, in themselves do not deserve it.

But what actually is Grace? In a nutshell, grace is the supernatural power to do that which we in our own strength are unable to do, which is an unmerited favour. We are given 'Grace' to live the life our Father wants us to live, that is a life in obedience to the teaching of Jesus His Son. To do this our Father has offered us His 'Grace', all we have to do is 'ASK'. Remember, 'you have not because you ask not', so ask. Also, 'you have not because you ask amiss', you ask not in accordance to the teaching of Jesus. So if you ask for His 'Grace' to live according to the teachings of Jesus, our Father is going to answer that request. Why?

First you ask, secondly, what you ask for must be according to His will, it must be in accordance to the teaching of Jesus, this is to be found in the Gospels. An example is asking His to guide you to begin to live like Jesus wants you to live, in accordance to His word.

Remember the two men who were building their houses? They probably had the same intention.

They both needed to build a house so they had somewhere to live. Their dreams were the same. Their longings were the same. Their desires were the same. Bishop Evans wrote; 'What marks these two men apart is that they view the future from different perspectives'. They both wanted to build a house.

The concept of building a house in its most immediate interpretation would be to erect a life, to build a life worth living, to build a life that is significant, to build a life that is going somewhere. You could relate it to building a future and building a family, since families live in homes, you could also say both men wanted to have vigorous, dynamic, strong households. Of course the church of Jesus Christ is called the household of faith (Galatians

6:10) so we could apply it to building a ministry and since the sustainability of our life worth living depends not only on the spiritual but also the financial aspect of our life, because you need a kind of income to survive, so we could also relate it to building a career or business.

You are probably building all four. You're building a life. You want a life that you are happy with, that God is pleased with, and that when you look back on it you are glad. You want a family that is strong and stable and vibrant, alive and committed. And you want a ministry that will stand the test of time, you also want a career or business empire that will enable you to fulfil your dreams, your purpose to God and your family. All of us fit into this brief story. Both men had the same intention and probably life wishes.

Both men received the same instruction.

Not only did both have the same intentions, they both also listened to the same lecture, because it says both men *"heard these words of mine."*

Both men went to the same classroom and had the same professor. You don't get any better than this, because in this case, the 'written word was communicated by the living Word'.

Jesus himself was and is still the teacher (are you studying His teachings today?). Both men were committed to listening to divine truth. Both men were committed to making themselves available to divine input. We're not talking about one man having a love for hearing the truth, and another man a total hatred for it. We're talking about both men exposing themselves to Scripture. So the comparison between these two men is that they have the same intention. They want to see things rise from the ground and go higher, probably a life, a family, a ministry, a business, a career or all of these. And they received the same instruction, the same instructor, as they avail themselves of divine truth.

Both men faced the same challenge (Test).

There's a third comparison. These men lived in the same area. They lived in the same neighbourhood because they were both affected by the same storm. The description of the storm is precisely the same in both cases, and affected both men. Both men were subject to the same storm, which meant they were reasonably close to each other. Everybody reading this book is affected by a storm. All of you are definitely affected by the negative realities of life, business, career, ministry or family. It may not be exactly the same, but one thing is true of us all, we do get rained on.

There are various types of storms in life:

Sometimes the storm roars in as you are affected by sickness or the fear of death. May be you have just learnt that you have cancer or another life-threatening disease. Perhaps a loved one will suddenly pass away. You may develop a nagging injury that refuses to heal.

Maybe you're beginning to feel your age and this gives you an unending discouragement. Times like these reveal the foundations of your life.

Sometimes we are affected by circumstantial storms.

There are circumstances when everything and everyone seems to plot against us and situation seems to go wrong, like the case of Job who woke up one fateful morning only to discover that everything he had ever worked for had disappeared, all his children died one day, infected with horrible sickness and lost the support of his wife! Everything seems to go wrong at once. These are situational storms.

Sometimes we are affected by relational storms.

This is when there is high tension between you and the people related to you. When a relationship has been strained to the breaking point — parent and child, husband and wife, friends and acquaintance, your boss, co-workers, etc. — your life will be stormy. David found himself in this situation, he had just came back from battle field, only to discover that all his family, his belongings and all the families of his soldiers has been taken captives, everybody turns their back on him even his soldiers threatens to stone him, what a stormy situation he experienced

"Now it happened, when David and his men came to Ziklag, on the third day, that the Amalekites had invaded the South and Ziklag, attacked Ziklag and burned it with fire, 2 and had taken captive the women and those who were there, from small to great; they did not kill anyone, but carried them away and went their way. 3 So David and his men came to the city, and there it was, burned with fire; and their wives, their sons, and their daughters had been taken captive. 4 Then David and the people who were with him, lifted up their voices and wept, until they had no more power to weep.

5 And David's two wives, Ahinoam the Jezreelitess, and Abigail the widow of Nabal the Carmelite, had been taken captive. 6 Now David was greatly distressed, for the people spoke of stoning him, because the soul of all the people was grieved, every man for his sons and his daughters. But David strengthened himself in the Lord his God."

(1 Samuel 30:1-6)

Sometimes the storm is a crushing personal loss.

You may lose a business or a job that not only provides income but also provides you with self-esteem and personal security. Your carefully built stock portfolio suddenly destroyed can be like great storm roaring through the comfortable life you have constructed. When you realize that you have not built up the security you counted on, everything in your life can crumble and expose the faulty foundations of your life.

Sometimes ours may be emotional storms.

These are often hidden on the surface. We have a nice smile, but inside we're seething and boiling in distress. Many times there's a storm going on inside of us that doesn't even show. Paralyzed by fear of insecurities, overcome by guilt. Raging with anger. Consumed with worry or jealousy. Battling with feelings of inadequacies, etc. Those are the emotional storms of life.

Sometimes, our foundation is tested by prosperity.

Prosperity breezes in like gentle quiet rain. At first you're convinced it will make your life better, healthy and fulfilled. But when prosperity keeps coming, it can develop into a large destructive force as damaging as a storm.

What you gain, not what you lose, often serves as the supreme test of your foundation. More men and women have been knocked off their spiritual foundation by great wealth than the opposite.

Note please, Jesus did not say IF the storm comes, He says WHEN the storm comes. Life is not always sunshine. Life is not always exciting. Life has its moments of tears, moments of challenges. We all share the good and progressive intention, we are all group of builders, we want to build something; same training, we want to hear something; and same storms, we all have to face something.

CHAPTER—5

The Group Of Builders

LET US TAKE some of these foundations one by one and see the effect the foundation could have in our lives;

The foundation you build about your life; There are numerous opportunities we have lost in life simply because we laid a wrong foundation about our lives . . . .

The Lord has given me great opportunities to travel to so many countries across the globe. Doors of opportunities has been opened to me to serve under and alongside various ministers and ministries and presently by His grace as a senior pastor and General Overseer, I have been given great access to vital information as a spiritual, marital and career counsellor which leads me to the conclusion that the genesis of the world's problems is attributed to the wrong foundations.

What I have been able to diagnose in many cases is that many people underestimate the importance of the foundational aspects of their lives, though they aspire for Marital, Spiritual and Financial breakthrough.

Everybody wants to be on top, having his or her dreams realised, as Mr A or Mr B, forgetting the fact that there is a story behind every glory. They look up to people's accomplishments without really taken a look down to where they are coming from.

Many want to be at the peak of the mountain of success when the ladder that conveys you to the peak of your success is not strong enough to withstand your weight of accomplishment, or the floor where it stands is not solid enough or the wall it leans on is not stable, you can be very certain that it will last but for a very short time.

So, when the Lord speaks about foundation in Matthew 7, He speaks of security, anybody that is security minded, should also be foundational minded, because it is the foundation that determines the security of any entity.

Every wise man or woman keeps security in mind before they enter into any serious marital relationship, before they choose a career, before they engage in business deals, before they enter in to the ministry, etc.

For years, security has been topping the annual budget of many countries from the United States and many countries all over the world, even the countries that is not rich enough to equip themselves militarily acquires it in exchange of their natural resources.

Security budget in the United States is by far higher than average entire yearly budget of many developing countries, but if only we can take time to take care of the foundation, the problem of security would not have given us so much concern, as the saying goes; prevention is better than cure.

Most of the war fought today be it Spiritual or conventional are preventable, if we had only be foundation conscious.

Most of the family crises engulfing many homes today are preventable, and many marriages would have been saved, if we had only been foundation conscious.

Many Businesses that fold up or went bankrupt would have been saved, if only they have been foundation conscious.

If the foundation of a ministry is not well laid, such ministry is bound to fall.

The church is void of genuine anointing today because of wrong foundations laid by some ministers, real spiritual authority could not be exercised because many ministers themselves are not submissive to authority, the urge to exercise authority without being submissive ourselves has destroyed the power of authority in the ministry, the evil in Lucifer is his hunger for power, wanting to exercise authority without being submissive to one. Note, the Scriptures says, God will only punish disobedience when your obedient is fulfilled.

(2 Corinthians 10:69).

If you are a rebellious minister who rebelled against the authority over you or you left your church with resentments, rebellious attitude or anger without receiving a blessing from your spiritual head (Pastor). I don't care what theological qualification you have, if you are not submissive to your head Pastor through whom God used to train you, counsels you, teach you godly principles and prays for you, and you finally leave with quarrels and did not receive his blessing, you are laying a wrong ministerial foundation which is bound to fall and your ministry will be a breeding ground and oasis for rebellious Christians.

Likewise, if you break a Church to build your ministry, you will suffer a lot of Church breaking along the way in your ministry The Scriptures says in Galatians 6:7 *"Be not deceived; God is not mocked: for whatsoever a man soweth, that shall he also reap.* (KJV) God's order of sowing and reaping must be fulfilled for He says *". . . While the earth remains, seedtime and harvest, and cold and heat, and summer and winter, and day and night shall not cease"*

(Genesis 8:22) KJV

Life is a reflection of our seed; if you don't know what you have sown, check what you are reaping.

Minister of God, the way you start your ministry will surely determine the way you will finish.

CHAPTER—6

The Contrast between Saul and David (Part 1)

I WILL LIKE TO compare these two men the Lord Jesus mention in his parable to two important characters in the Bible, King Saul and King David, they will remain one of our example of foundation as we explore this book.

Both of them received a divine call from God to serve Him by leading the people of Israel

Both of them attended the same school of the Ministry under their sole spiritual teacher, mentor and father in the name of Samuel the prophet.

Both of them were equally prepared and well trained to succeed yet one ended by losing his crown, his throne and his God's given glory and the other ended as a prophet and a man whose heart is after the heart of God.

THE CRISES OF LEADERSHIP

Since the children of Israel came out of Egypt, God has been leading them every step of the way until the foundation was destroyed by the by the spiritual leaders appointed as judges in the land of Israel, First the children of Eli and later the children of Samuel.

A man might be on the whole a good man, and yet be marked by some defect, which mars his character and prevents his usefulness. A defect that makes him the unintentional cause of much grief.

Eli was such a man. He was a descendant of Ithamar, the youngest son of Aaron. He held the office of high priest and judge and also helped to raise Samuel.

You see things were not going right in the land of Israel. As the case would be over and over again in their history, they thought things were all right but just below the surface there was an illness, a cancer that needed to be dealt with, cut out. Right at the centre of their life together, in the Temple, their worship had been corrupted. And worse than that, the source of that corruption was the family of Eli, the High Priest. Eli knew what was going on but he did nothing about it.

The problems of Eli started because of his failure to discipline and raise his children in a godly way, they perverted justice, raped women who came to worship and took bribe thereby destroys the foundation laid by his forefathers.

"Now the sons of Eli were corrupt; they did not know the Lord. 13 And the priests' custom with the people was that when any man offered a sacrifice, the priest's servant would come with a three-pronged flesh hook in his hand while the meat was boiling. 14 Then he would thrust it into the pan, or kettle, or caldron, or pot; and the priest would take for himself all that the flesh hook brought up. So they did in Shiloh to all the Israelites who came there. 15 Also, before they burned the fat, the priest's servant would come and say to the man who sacrificed, "Give meat for roasting

to the priest, for he will not take boiled meat from you, but raw. 16 And if the man said to him, "They should really burn the fat first; then you may take as much as your heart desires," he would then answer him, "No, but you must give it now; and if not, I will take it by force." 17 Therefore the sin of the young men was very great before the Lord, for men abhorred the offering of the Lord.

(1 Samuel 2:17)

This matter displeased the Lord, for He saw that the foundation of holiness, justice, freedom and fairness which was laid for their father to dwell and to build on is being destroyed and Eli did nothing about it and God therefore stepped in.

"Therefore Eli said unto Samuel, Go, lie down: and it shall be, if he call thee, that thou shalt say, Speak, Lord; for thy servant heareth. So Samuel went and lay down in his place. 10 And the Lord came, and stood, and called as at other times, Samuel, Samuel. Then Samuel answered, Speak; for thy servant heareth. 11 And the Lord said to Samuel, Behold, I will do a thing in Israel, at which both the ears of every one that heareth it shall tingle. 12 In that day I will perform against Eli all things which I have spoken concerning his house: when I begin, I will also make an end. 13 For I have told him that I will judge his house for ever for the iniquity which he knoweth; because his sons made themselves vile, and he restrained them not. 14 And therefore I have sworn unto the house of Eli, that the iniquity of Eli's house shall not be purged with sacrifice nor offering forever"

(1 Samuel 3:9-14)

God pointed out to Eli that he had failed to restrain his children from this godless act of blasphemy, he and his family line were to be all wiped out. The priesthood ministry that had been theirs since the days of Moses and Aaron was to be taken away and given to another. Even though God had promised that Eli's house would minister before him forever, it wouldn't happen, the foundation of priesthood has just being destroyed.

Their failure was too great. In fact their failure is just another example of the continuing failure of family lines to maintain faithfulness to God through the generations.

And God said "Then I will raise up for Myself a faithful priest who shall do according to what is in My heart and in My mind. I will build him a sure house, and he shall walk before My anointed forever. (1 Samuel 2:35) and that was fulfilled in the sons Zadok who lives an exemplary life of faithfulness, unlike the sons of Eli, even when the whole land went astray they kept the faith

[5]*"But the priests, the Levites, the sons of Zadok, who kept charge of My sanctuary when the children of Israel went astray from Me, they shall come near Me to minister to Me; and they shall stand before Me to offer to Me the fat and the blood," says the Lord GOD.* [16] *"They shall enter My sanctuary, and they shall come near My table to minister to Me, and they shall keep My charge"*

(Ezekiel 44:15-16

Consequently, the children of Israel lost the war they should have won, the Ark of covenant, the powerhouse of Israel, was captured by the enemies.

Whenever we fail to carry out our responsibilities at home or in our ministry, whenever our families turns their back to God and we feel indifferent about it, the consequences can be greater than we could ever imagine, because our attitude affects our foundation, and where the foundation of our marriage or ministry has been destroyed, it simply opens the back door to the enemies just as we have read over here, to enter and kill, steal and destroy (John 10:10).

Whenever the foundation of any family is destroyed as a result of negligence to maintain our spiritual foundation, the back door is always automatically left opened and the enemy will come in and kill the marriage, steal their joy and destroy the family.

If we also disregard the word of God, we are going to be disregarded, God disregarded Eli, he was not only blind physically, he was also blind spiritually, his disregard to God's word also led to his spiritual deafness, if we disregard the word of God, God will bypass us to communicate His will and purpose to another person that is willing to hear, respect and obey the His word.

Have you been too busy to take care of some little anomalies in your family? Are you afraid of confronting some important issues springing up in your family, your business or your ministry?

Check the end of Eli, his sin was that he simply failed to correct his children when they are correctable and bend them when they are bendable, he actually tried to caution them latter, but it was too late.

Note this: If you don't bend a tree when it's fresh and bendable, if you wait until it becomes dry, any effort to bend it latter will break it.

"Now Eli was very old; and he heard everything his sons did to all Israel, [c] and how they lay with the women who assembled at the door of the tabernacle of meeting. 23 So he said to them, "Why do you do such things? For I hear of your evil dealings from

all the people. 24 No, my sons! For it is not a good report that I hear. You make the Lord's people transgress. 25 If one man sins against another, God will judge him. But if a man sins against the Lord, who will intercede for him?" Nevertheless they did not heed the voice of their father, because the Lord desired to kill them
(1 Samuel 2:25)

The Consequences; It led to the seizure of the Ark of God, Eli's two sons Hophni and Phinehas who are the perpetrators of the act both died the same day;

"So the Philistines fought, and Israel was defeated, and every man fled to his tent. There was a very great slaughter, and there fell of Israel thirty thousand foot soldiers. Also the ark of God was captured; and the two sons of Eli, Hophni and Phinehas, died.
(1 Samuel 4:10-11)

And ultimately, Eli, died as a result of the bad news he heard. So the messenger answered and said, "Israel has fled before the Philistines, and there has been a great slaughter among the people. Also your two sons, Hophni and Phinehas, are dead; and the ark of God has been captured. *"Then it happened, when he made mention of the ark of God, that Eli fell off the seat backward by the side of the gate; and his neck was broken and he died, for the man was old and heavy. And he had judged Israel forty years"*
(1 Samuel 4:16-17)

So the end of Eli and his two sons came tragically on the same day

The failure of the children of Eli led to God's choice of Samuel, the prophet of the most high, a loving priest, an intercessor and mentor.

The same thing that befell the house of Eli also affected the family of Samuel, the difference here is that God did not blame him for not correcting or restraining his children, probably he has done all he could to put them right and his sons simply refused to change, unlike Eli, but whichever way it is, it does not serve as justification the neglect of our responsibilities towards our children.

As a result of leadership decay, fear of insecurity, fairness of justice as a result of ungodly behaviour of the children of Samuel, spiritual declension and the growing desire to be like other nation led the children of Israel to reject the judges and demand for a king.

We can see the foundation being destroyed over here, if we refuse to walk in the ways of the Lord, we will lose the protection, support, the respect and the favour, which God granted us among men.

"Then all the elders of Israel gathered themselves together, and came to Samuel unto Ramah, and said unto him, Behold, thou art old, and thy sons walk not in thy ways: now make us a king to judge us like all the nations 1Samuel 8:4-5)

Samuel was initially sad at the request of the elders representing the people of Israel, but God asked Samuel to harken to the demand of His people the result of which Saul was called and anointed as the first king in the history of the Israelites.

The foundation was destroyed, when the children of Israel, because of the leadership problem, rejected God as their King and demanded for the one that will lead them to the warfront just like other nations, they have forgotten that they are not other people, they are the people of God, they forgot that they had no king nor the army captain when God destroyed the Egyptian army for their sake, they fought the Amalekite and overcame them, they conquered the giants in Canaan, they overcame the wall of Jericho, they were able to possess the land God apportioned to them through their fore father, none of this was accomplished through a king, for God has always been their king, for He said;

"O Israel, you are destroyed, But your help is from Me I will be your King; Where is any other, That he may save you in all your cities? And your judges, to whom you said, 'Give me a king and princes'? I gave you a king in My anger, And took him away in My wrath"
(Hosea 13:9-11)

We should not allow the pressures of the world and the challenges we are experiencing to change our focus from God and we should not chose the visible option over the invisible authority over us thereby losing the precious relationship between us and the Lord.

There are times, when we claim that we are Christians and God is our king, but our attitudes speaks the direct opposite, we reject His ways, we reject His precepts, we rebel against His authority, but we say we don't reject the Lord as our King but remember whenever God is not permitted to rule, He overrules to accomplish His divine purpose.

CHAPTER—7

The Contrast between Saul and David (Part 2)

The Call of Saul

WHILE SAUL WAS looking for his father's lost donkeys, he went to Samuel to inquire where the lost donkeys could be, but later discovered that the loss of the donkeys could as well be the plan of God, because his disappointment led to discovery of the divine plan of God for him and his discovery eventually led to the recovery of the missing donkeys! Remember *". . . all things work together for good to those who love God, to those who are the called according to His purpose."*

(Romans 8:28)

Saul was called according to God's purpose and he discovered God's appointment in his disappointment over the failure to locate the where about of his father's ass. Our God is God of blessed appointment.

Saul actually received a divine call from God, though the Israelite rejected God's leadership and demanded for a king to lead them like other nations, they did not specifically chose Saul; God gave Saul to them in answer to their demand.

God established a relationship with Saul, handed him over to his pastor and mentor Samuel, just as Saul of Tarsus as well-known as Paul was handed over to Ananias.

(Acts 9:10-19)

1. After he has been anointed as the king,

He received divine assurances that confirms his call and established him as God's servant and leader of God's people

"When you have departed from me today, you will find two men by Rachel's tomb in the territory of Benjamin at Zelzah; and they will say to you, 'The donkeys which you went to look for have been found. And now your father has ceased caring about the donkeys and is worrying about you, saying, "What shall I do about my son?"

(1 Samuel 10:2)

When Saul answered the call of God, **his spiritual, financial and material needs were met**, if you have received a call to the place of leadership and you are worried over having your needs met, If truly God has called you, He will meet with your needs.

2. He will receive the Bread of life (Jesus Christ)

"Then you shall go on forward from there and come to the terebinth tree of Tabor. There three men going up to God at Bethel will meet you, one carrying three young goats, another carrying three loaves of bread, and another carrying a skin of wine. ⁴And

they will greet you and give you two loaves of bread, which you shall receive from their hands."

(1 Samuel 10:3-4)

I believe the three loaves of bread stands for the Trinity — Father, Son and the Holy Spirit, bread also stand for the name of Jesus, as He declared;

"I am the bread of life, he who comes to me shall never hunger and he who believes in Me shall never thirst."

(John 6:3)

So, as Saul receives the bread, He was receiving Christ.

Also Jesus said, he will never hunger, that is another assurance of God's provision, all the provisions needed by the new King will be supplied (Philippians 4:19) God who calls you will equip you and the one who anoints you will provide for you.

3. God supplied him with the spiritual power needed to lead God's people,

He would come to the hill of the Lord and meet the prophet, and the Spirit of the Lord shall come upon him, king Saul received the power of the Holy Spirit and the gift of prophecy in vs. 9 ". . . as he turned back from Samuel, God gave him another heart, Saul was saved, God removed from him a heart of stone and gave him a heart of flesh and Saul turned to another man

"After that you shall come to the hill of God where the Philistine garrison is. And it will happen, when you have come there to the city, that you will meet a group of prophets coming down from the

high place with a stringed instrument, a tambourine, a flute, and a harp before them; and they will be prophesying.⁶ Then the Spirit of the Lord will come upon you, and you will prophesy with them and be turned into another man.

(1 Samuel 10:5-7).

4. God also gave him an assurance that He will be with him,

God will be with us as long as we remain in His will ".⁷ And let it be, when these signs come to you, that you do as the occasion demands; for God is with you."

(1 Samuel 10:7)

5. God would provide the people

"And Saul also went home to Gibeah; and valiant men went with him, whose hearts God had touched."

(1 Samuel 10: 26)

A King is going to need committed and dedicated people, God gave him people whose heart has been touched, people who will love Saul and be committed to serve and protect him.

If God truly has called you to the ministry, He will touch the heart of men to bless you, you don't need to play games or use any manipulations.

"Faithful is he that calleth you, who also will do it."
(1 Thessalonians 5:24) **KJV**

If you are serving the Lord, He will give you all that is needed to succeed in the ministry, He will solve your problems, He will give necessary provisions, provide the spiritual power, give you the assurance of His presence with you and touch the heart of the people to serve and bless you.

In spite of all these wonderful beginnings, Saul failed woefully, he started by following the Lord and he finished by following the devil

He truly had a solid Godly foundation, God built an excellent relationship with him, but he failed to maintain it.

The fall of Saul

He began to fall when he shifted his focus from God and his ordained authority, he expected Samuel to come and offer the necessary sacrifice and when Samuel seems to have delayed more than necessary, he left his throne and took over the position of a priest, he does not know that the fact that he prophesied does not make him a prophet.

Likewise, many may think that because they are able to preach well, God has qualified them to be a pastor, they have forgotten that to preach is a gift, however, to be a pastor is a calling which carries such responsibility, those who are called will answer to Jesus for how they have functioned in such a role of responsibility.

All pastors are preachers but not all preachers are pastors.

When he was confronted on why he does it he said;

"And Samuel said, "What have you done?"

Saul said, "When I saw that the people were scattered from me, and that you did not come within the days appointed, and that the Philistines gathered together at Michmash,

(1 Samuel 13:11)

Everybody seems to have a share of the blame but Saul

When Saul began to walk by sight and not by faith he began to get into trouble and he suddenly knew that he was facing a large army; his soldier were abandoning him, they were hedged and in distress, they were trembling and scattered.

The storms revealed the state of Saul's foundation

He blamed Samuel for coming late and he blamed the people for scattering from him, he has forgotten the word of God that says *"And let it be, when these signs come to you, that you do as the occasion demands; for God is with you."*(1Samuel 10:7), even if everybody scatters and you have God, you have everything you need.

Latter he began to fight a wrong battle, when a believer is not following the Lord, he will treat his friend like enemies and enemies as friends. He was fighting David instead of the devil, many Churches like Saul, have left a good fight of faith to fight a bad fight of the flesh.

They have abandoned the call to resist the devil and instead focus their fight with the Saints, they have replaced power with politics and gossip is getting more popular than 'Gospel.'

Samuel said; you have done foolishly. Warren W. Wiersbe said" It is foolish to fear the enemy instead of God. It is foolish to run ahead of God and try to tell Him what to do. It is foolish to be dishonest and lie about your sins.

If anyone had a reason to succeed, it was Saul, yet he failed woefully. In the beginning, he had almost everything in his favour.

He had a divine call from God, he had the power of the Holy Spirit (Anointing) to accomplish God's purpose, he had a wonderful praying friend in Samuel the prophet, he had a group of loyal men to help and support him, yet he failed.

What excuses do you have for failing to accomplish God's purpose, authorities have been giving to us,(Mark 16:17-19), you have the power of the Holy Spirit and probably blessed with a good pastor.

After series of failures and disappointment, God gave him another chance.

Samuel said to Saul in 1 Samuel 15:1-3 *"Samuel also said to Saul, "The Lord sent me to anoint you king over His people, over Israel. Now therefore, heed the voice of the words of the Lord. Thus says the Lord of hosts: 'I will punish Amalek for what he did to Israel, how he ambushed him on the way when he came up from Egypt. Now go and attack Amalek, and utterly destroy all that they have, and do not spare them. But kill both man and woman, infant and nursing child, ox and sheep, camel and donkey."*

God gave him an instruction, yet instead of total obedience, he started giving excuses, he replaced words for action, the instruction given to him was to completely destroy the Amalekite, the longtime enemy of Israel, he went as commanded by God but carried out things in his own ways.

He spared Agag, the Amalekite King, and all that was good in his eyes and destroys everything despised and worthless (vs.9) He used the gift God has given to him to promote and built a monument for himself, while Samuel was praying and crying for him he was busy promoting and receiving praise for himself.

The more Saul was elevated, the greater the moral decline until God said in 1 Samuel 15: 11 that "I greatly regret that I have set up Saul as king, for he has turned back from following Me, and has not performed My commandments. And it grieved Samuel, and he cried out to the Lord all night."

And God said further *"So Samuel said, "When you were little in your own eyes, were you not head of the tribes of Israel? And did not the Lord anoint you king over Israel?*

(1 Samuel 15:11)

Many times, we often forget where the Lord has taken us from, when we were nobody, He made us somebody, he puts our feet on the pathway of success, even though we are not yet what He wants us to be, but we should always remember that we are no longer what we used to be, and hence be grateful to God, every day of our lives. God is disappointed when we disobey Him and rebel against His authority, for any disobedience to the word of God is rebellion against His person. Foundation of our relationship is maintained by our obedience to His word.

When confronted by Samuel, Saul replied by saying; *"but I have obeyed the voice of the Lord and gone on a mission which He sent me . . . but the people took of the plunder"*, not Saul, *but the people . . .* (Vs. 20-21) Again he shifted blame; a man who is good at giving excuse is good for nothing.

How many times have you said the same thing, replacing saying for doing. It is so easy for the people of God to replace action for words but God does not want words in place of actions, He does not want excuses instead of confession, He doesn't want self-justification instead of a sense of remorse and repentance.

Saul gave excuses instead of confession, does he sound like you? He has never assume responsibility for his actions, he always blame somebody for his acts

Saul said

"And Saul said, "They have brought them from the Amalekites; for the people spared the best of the sheep and the oxen, to sacrifice to the Lord your God; and the rest we have utterly destroyed."

(1 Samuel 15; 15)

"So Samuel said:
"Has the Lord as great delight in burnt offerings and sacrifices,
As in obeying the voice of the Lord?
Behold, to obey is better than sacrifice,
And to heed than the fat of rams.
²⁵ For rebellion is as the sin of witchcraft,
And stubbornness is as iniquity and idolatry.
Because you have rejected the word of the Lord,
He also has rejected you from being king."

(1 Samuel 15:22-23)

Saul was more concerned about sacrifice rather than obedience, but God does not need our sacrifice, He would rather have our obedience

"For I desire mercy and not sacrifice, and the knowledge of God more than burnt offerings.

(Hosea 6:6)

Moreover, the Psalmist wrote in Psalm 50:12-14

"If I were hungry, I would not tell you;
For the world is Mine, and all its fullness.
Will I eat the flesh of bulls,
Or drink the blood of goats?
Offer to God thanksgiving,
And pay your vows to the Most High"

Also, the statement of Saul revealed that He had no personal relationship with God anymore after the experience at the hill of the Lord (I Samuel 10:5) he has never spent time to build his foundation of relationship with God, He said . . . to sacrifice to the Lord **your** God and not **his** God.

Everybody is responsible to build his or her relationship with God; a foundation is of no use if no structure is constructed on it.

After Saul has received the sentence over his rebellious attitude, he begged Samuel (Not God) and the reason is that Samuel might honour him in the presence of the people (Not to intercede for him in the presence of God) "Then he said, *"I have sinned; yet honour me now, please, before the elders of my people and before Israel, and return with me, that I may worship the Lord your God." ³¹ So Samuel turned back after Saul, and Saul worshiped the Lord.*

(1 Samuel 15:30)

Saul was concern about his reputation with the people rather than his character and his relationship with God

The reputation that we have, is what men thinks that we are, men that goes after reputation does things to impress people, and are ready to do anything to earn their reputation, that is the world of politics.

Reputation is a mask worn to look good to the world, but there is a difference between looking good and being really good. Reputation is a valuable asset to the godless and they are ready to do anything to protect and maintain it.

God knows us not by our reputation but by our character. Moody wrote; "Character is what you are in the dark, when you are alone, when nobody sees you".

Are we people of reputation or are we people of character? Are we fighting to protect our reputation or maintain our character?

The Scriptures says in Romans 12:2 . . . "Do not be conformed to this world, but be ye transformed . . ."

Conformity is the way of the world; you are not a popular man if you are not conforming to the ways of the world.

You don't really have to go along to be able to get along.

Be a God pleaser and not a man pleaser. Saul prefers to be a man of the people than to be a man of God. Don't live for people, live for God, don't fear people or worry about receiving the honour from men,

". . . *Fear God, and keep his commandments: for this is the whole duty of man.[14] For God shall bring every work into judgment, with every secret thing, whether it be good, or whether it be evil.* (Ecclesiastes 12:13-14), be a man of integrity. Jesus said "*Woe to you when all men speak well of you, for so did their fathers to the false prophets.* (Luke 6:26)

The foundation was destroyed and Saul did nothing about it, he was neither repentant nor remorseful, as a result of this, God rejected him from being king over His people.

"*Now the Lord said to Samuel, "How long will you mourn for Saul, seeing I have rejected him from reigning over Israel? Fill your horn with oil, and go; I am sending you to Jesse the Bethlehemite. For I have provided Myself a king among his sons."*
(1 Samuel 16:1)

Some ministers are like King Saul, they are careless of their foundation, they have placed themselves higher than anyone one could approach, advice or correct them, they would not listen to warnings or advice, their compromise and continuous unrepentant attitude has led to God rejecting them and their ministry, even though they still have a huge crowd of people, it is not enough yardstick to measure the state of their spiritual foundation even Satan himself can attract a larger crowd.

CHAPTER—8

The Contrast between Saul and David (Part 3)

David, a Man after God's Heart

David was anointed in his stead, *"Then Samuel took the horn of oil and anointed him in the midst of his brothers; and the Spirit of the Lord came upon David from that day forward. So Samuel arose and went to Ramah.*

(1Samuel 16:13).

The Spirit of God came upon David and the Spirit of God left Saul. *"But the Spirit of the Lord departed from Saul, and a distressing spirit from the Lord troubled him."*

(1Samuel 16:14).

The presence of the Spirit of God is a sign of God's presence with David and the sign of the Spirit of God leaving Saul is a sign of God's rejection of Saul.

David fought more battles than any king in the history of the whole land of Israel, and he lost no battle, have you ever wondered why? Because he maintained a good spiritual foundation.

David was serving God under King Saul, David was not only talented he was also anointed, whenever he plays his musical Instrument, King Saul receives deliverance from his demonic oppression.

"And so it was, whenever the spirit from God was upon Saul, that David would take a harp and plays it with his hand. Then Saul would become refreshed and well, and the distressing spirit would depart from him"

(1 Samuel 16:23)

Saul loved David greatly until the spirit of envy possessed him and he hated him to the extent that he wanted to kill him. Saul eventually exiled David for winning the war that he the King could not win.

Love can turn to hatred even to murder when pride poisons our heart and envy controls our emotions.

When the hand of God is on your life, the world's attention will certainly be drawn to you, after the killing of Goliath, he became the talk of the town, he was being praised for killing ten thousand and Saul a thousand, the spirit of pride in Saul made him to forget that they were both doing the work of God, he does not seem to know that "Paul may plant and Apollo waters, It is only God that gives the increase" (I Corinthians 3:7)

There are actually some men of God who are like King Saul, who think like King Saul, sees like King Saul and act like King Saul, who see every minister working under them as their personal belonging and sub-ministers and believe that God will have to move only through them, who feel threatened by sudden growth and popularity of their spiritual sons forgetting the fact that whatever achievements they might have accomplished, it is all to the glory of God.

Envy is like a cancer of the soul, when you allow yourself to become jealous of another man's possession or accomplishments, envy will consume you until it takes complete control of your life and begins to destroy you.

Envy is one of the oldest sins in the world; remember it was envy that led Cain to kill Abel. Envy is a destroyer, if you allow it in your life, it can lead you to commit great sin of extreme hatred, crime, kill or be killed.

David became a fugitive in a foreign land, King Saul still chased after him.

It was foolish of Saul trying to kill David, because David is God's anointed.

"The wicked watches the righteous, and seeks to slay him.[33] The LORD will not leave him in his hand,
Nor condemn him when he is judged"
(Psalms 37:32-33).

With the hand of God upon your life, the enemy cannot prevail over you for God watches over your soul. The Scripture says:

"For the eyes of the LORD run to and fro throughout the whole earth, to show Himself strong on behalf of those whose heart is loyal to Him"
(2 Chronicles 16:9)

All these situations brought the best in David and worst in Saul.

God's permitted trials in your life is not intended to destroy you but to build you and draw you even closer to Him, if you put your trust in Him.

David's Ultimate weapon

While Saul was on the Chase of David to kill him, God turned the situation around and handed Saul over to David

"So David took the spear and the jug of water by Saul's head, and they got away; and no man saw or knew it or awoke. For they were all asleep, because **a deep sleep from the Lord** *had fallen on them"*
(1 Samuel 24 & 26)

On two different occasions, David had the opportunity to kill King Saul. From a human point of view, the death of King Saul would have solved many or all the problems that David had at that moment, after all, the enemy is gone now and the throne automatically becomes David's throne, and that will hasten the fulfilment of the word of God.

What would you have done if you were in David's shoes?

Firstly, Of course, many would have gladly take him out of the way, after all he is your enemy who wanted you dead and you have done it in self defence

Secondly, we would have done it to hasten the fulfilment of the word of the Lord in our lives, in other words, helping God to do His work in our own way and time, remembering that it was God Himself who put him to sleep. ". . . For they were all asleep, **because a deep sleep from the LORD** had fallen on them.
(1 Samuel 26:12)

David was encouraged by his men to kill King Saul; they even quoted the word of God!

Then the men of David said to him, *"This is the day of which the LORD said to you, 'Behold, I will deliver your enemy into your hand that you may do to him as it seems good to you.'" And David arose and secretly cut off a corner of Saul's robe.*

(1 Samuel 24:4)

Sometimes, wrong application of the word of God often misleads many people.

Almost everybody can always wrongfully quote the word of God to suit their purpose and to justify their acts, just as the unrepentant drunkards always find the Scripture to back themselves, so also the fornicator and smokers also find a passage to justify their acts.

After all, Samuel has said that God has rejected Saul "But Samuel said to Saul, "I will not return with you, for you have rejected the word of the LORD, and the LORD has rejected you from being king over Israel." (1 Samuel 15:6), and Jonathan said the Lord would cut off the enemies of David *"but you shall not cut off your kindness from my house forever, no, not when the LORD has cut off every one of the enemies of David from the face of the earth."*

(1 Samuel 20:15)

Either of these could have given David the right to kill King Saul.

David did not yield to this temptation because to begin with, he realised that Saul was not his enemy, David might have been Saul's enemy but David is not an enemy with Saul

David in the valley of decision.

David is confronted here with one of the greatest challenges of his life.

Beloved, when you are exposed to situations, it gives you options, and option gives you choices and choices requires your decision.

David was faced with an option to revenge or restrain, David decided to choose the latter, instead of revenge, he chose to restrain himself and his men. The opportunity or temptation of revenge seems as God's provision, but watch out!

The Devil also sets a trap through it, watch out when you seem to have received a 'rhema word' from God or when the blessings of God come presenting itself to you, Satan also sets a trap through it, so that your blessing might be infected with spiritual viruses that can damage your relationship with God, thereby hindering your blessings.

Who or what is your greatest influence in your moment of decision? Is it the word of God or the state of the situations?

Restrain is a great sign of maturity.

The way we respond to situation reveals our level of maturity.

There are lots of lessons to learn from David, as David showed restrain we also need to show restraint in all our ways, our family, our relationship with other people, our spending, our reactions to injustices, etc.

David possesses an attribute that God is looking for in all of His people, self-control, which is one of the principal fruit of the Spirit (Galatians 5:23).

What role can self-control play in your daily life? Have you faced any challenge in the past where self-control plays a decisive role and served as a principal key to your success or safety?

Through his attitude, David proved the kind of great man he was. Proverb 16:32 says "He who is slow to anger is better than the mighty, and he who rules his spirit than he who takes a city"

David proved that he was truly a king by ruling and reigning over his own will and emotions.

You are faced each day with challenges that put your maturity to test.

If you cannot rule over your will and emotions, you are not fit to be a leader, be it of a Church, family, country or community.

There is a story of a pastor who has just finished preaching on 'putting your old man to death', soon after the service, one of the member went quietly to tempt him, holding the cup of cold water in his hand and suddenly spilled it on the pastor, the pastor flared up immediately and the member said, Pastor, I thought your old man is dead but now I can see that your old man is not dead but sleeping and I have succeeded in waking it up with ordinary cup of water!

It is also very unfortunate that many Christian's old man is not dead but sleeping, and can be easily stirred up by any little provocation.

David was a fruit bearing son of God, before we lead the people we ought to lead ourselves, and before we rule the people we ought to rule over our emotions. For "the Spirit of the prophet is subject to the prophet" (1 Corithians14:32).

If he had not controlled his emotions and ruled his spirit, he would have killed King Saul; hence, a wrong foundation would have been laid.

What kept David from taking revenge against Saul?

1: Respect for the authority. He called him `My master` the anointed of the Lord (1 Samuel 24:6)
2: David respected the fact that King Saul was God's anointed
3: He also called him the King (vs.8)
4: He also called him my Father (vs.11)

The Scriptures says; *Let every soul be subject to the governing authorities. For there is no authority except from God, and the authorities that exist are appointed by God. 2 Therefore whoever resists the authority resists the ordinance of God, and those who resist will bring judgment on themselves* (Romans 13: 1-2)

1 Samuel 26:6-11 clearly reveals the depth of David's respect for the anointed of the Lord *"Then David answered, and said to Ahimelech the Hittite and to Abishai the son of Zeruiah, brother of Joab, saying, "Who will go down with me to Saul in the camp?" And Abishai said, "I will go down with you." So David and Abishai came to the people by night; and there Saul lay sleeping within the camp, with his spear stuck in the ground by his head. And Abner and the people lay all around him. ⁸ Then Abishai said to David, "God has delivered your enemy into your hand this day. Now therefore, please, let me strike him at once with the spear, right to the earth; and I will not have to strike him a second time!"*

But David said to Abishai, "Do not destroy him; for who can stretch out his hand against the LORD's anointed, and be guiltless?" ¹⁰ David said furthermore, "As the LORD lives, the LORD shall strike him, or his day shall come to die, or he shall go out to battle and perish. ¹¹ The LORD forbid that I should stretch out my hand against the LORD's anointed. But please, take now the spear and the jug of water that are by his head, and let us go."

David knew the mind of God, God said through this personal knowledge with King Saul; he was able to express the mind of God in one of his Psalms;

"He permitted no one to do them wrong;
Yes, He rebuked kings for their sakes,
Saying, "Do not touch My anointed ones, And do My prophets no harm."
(Psalm 105:14-15)

Note, If David had killed King Saul, what would have been the consequences, (Galatians 6:7)

David knew the mind of God and abides in His will, a lot of people including his son Absalom conspired against him to kill him, but God permitted no one to do him wrong, and God also rebuked the Kings for his sake, (Psalm 105:14-15) he enjoyed God's absolute protection, he fought more wars than any king in the land of Israel and lost no battle, because he maintained a right foundation. You can also enjoy this kind of protection if you maintain a right relationship with God for His word says *"Delight yourself also in the LORD, and He shall give you the desires of your heart.*

(Psalm 37:4)

King Saul's attitude has destroyed the relationship he had with God, because he neglected and failed to maintain the Foundation he had with God. We are living in a stormy world, the world that is full of test and trials we need a kind of strong and Solid foundation to be able to withstand the test of time, Saul probably taught he wasn't going to need

God or Samuel again, remember that Samuel has left him and God has taken His Spirit from him, he was actually dead before he finally dies.

Since the only relationship he had was with Samuel and not with God, he has neglected the spiritual benefits to seek after the worldly gains; he has abandoned the group of the prophets to embrace the group of ungodly. Samuel has died and his only means of communication with God has gone and now the need arises for him to hear from God. That sounds like many people who only remember God in time of crises, they only go to church when they are in need and they only pray when they are in trouble.

He went to enquire from God, with whom he had no relationship, he taught God is a kind of fixer who fixes problems, he does not know that the bible says *"If I hid iniquity in my heart, the Lord will not hear me"* (Psalm 66:18) So the Lord did not answer him neither by dreams or Urim and Saul immediately came with plan B.

Faith has no alternative, but Saul had an alternative because he was a man of flesh and not of faith, he quickly remembered one of the witches he has put away during his early days on the throne, he put them out of his sight but not out of his mind, just like many Christians do today, they are receiving Christ without letting go of the world, they leave the sinful back door to their past life opened just in case things doesn't work according to their expectations, they still keep the contacts of all the people and places that will serve as their worldly refuge in case the church doesn't meet their expectations. Many people are changing Churches and not their hearts.

After your salvation what are you still doing with the phone numbers of your ex-boyfriends and ex-girlfriends? The bad companies you have denounced, why are you keeping their contact numbers? Those wears you have turned your back to, why are you still keeping them in your wardrobes?

Both Saul and David experienced storms in their lives, both of them faced challenges; both of them were tested and tempted, both of them fell into temptation and their foundations served as a determine factor of their success or failure.

CHAPTER—9

The place of Patience is Building on a right foundation

The two men possessed two different characters

Like David and Saul, there is definitely something that differentiates the two characters Jesus talked about, from one another. To begin with, they possessed two different characters.

The first man was called a wise man, while the second was called foolish. One is considered wise; a wise man who considered building something, a wise man that acquired a spiritual training, one who is wise in the storm.

The other is considered a foolish man who planned of building something, one who exposes himself to divine truth, one who acted foolishly in a storm.

Wisdom is a deep understanding and realization of people, things, events or situations, resulting in the ability to apply perceptions and divine truth, judgements and actions in keeping with this understanding.

The fool in this passage is not necessarily the person who lacks information, but the person who does little or virtually nothing with the information received. Just like Saul and Gehazi, as you will discover latter in my illustrations that they equally received sufficient information; yet, they were still fundamentally different from David and Elisha. Make no mistake, both of them had dreams. They both had training, both also had storms. Outwardly, they would have looked like twins, but according to the Scriptures, fundamentally they were different men.

The two men built on different foundations

What are the fundamental differences between these two men?

The type and the geographical location of the foundations they had constructed, which states that the wise man built his house upon the rock, and the foolish man built his house upon the sand. While both men have the same intention, while both men have the same dream, the same instructor and experienced the same storm, their foundation is not the same. The security of their dreams, of their training, and of their trials was different.

What differentiates the building on a foundation of rock and building on a foundation of sand? What were the two thinking that made one a fool and one a wise man? According to the Lord Jesus in the Book of Luke 6:48, which says the wise man dug deep. As I have said, building on the rock can be very costly; you can build on sand fairly cheaply. To build on rock is hard work; to build on sand takes short time.

One builder patiently endured the pain, the time, the cost and the difficulty of breaking the stones to be able to lay his foundation on the rock, while the other ignored the fundamental rule of construction, took the shortcut which is faster, easier and at a reduced cost to build on sand.

Many people will like to lay a strong foundation but very few can actually pay the price involved. Our present world is based on the fast lane. While people seem to be conscious about their security, preference is still given to the speed above the security. Many more people prefer fast food, fast cars, fast planes, fast lane and even microwave prayer etc. We shouldn't forget that the faster it goes, the bigger the crash.

Impatience is a clear sign of immaturity and foolishness, It takes patience to obtain a good career, find a good wife or a good husband. For example, it took, Jacob 14 years to marry Rachel *"And Jacob served seven years for Rachel; and they seemed unto him but a few days, for the love he had to her.* (Genesis 29:20).

It takes patience to build a lasting business empire, it takes patience to raise children, it takes patience to receive answers to our prayers, *"And we desire that every one of you do shew the same diligence to the full assurance of hope unto the end: That ye be not slothful, but followers of them who through faith and patience inherit the promises"* (Hebrew 6:11-12) and (Hebrew 10:36) *"For ye have need of patience, that, after ye have done the will of God, ye might receive the promise.*

It takes great patient for Abraham to receive the promise, it took Patience for Noah to construct the ark, there is unfortunately no microwave Christianity, we have to work out our salvation with fear and trembling as the Scriptures says *"And so, after he had patiently endured, he obtained the promise* (Hebrew 6:15).

Our God is a God of patience; *"Be patient therefore, brethren, unto the coming of the Lord. Behold, the husbandman waiteth for the precious fruit of the earth, and hath long patience for it, until he receive the early and latter rain"* (James 5:7-8), no wonder patience is an indispensable part of the fruits of the Spirit.

No lasting or successful business is built without patience, without patience, endurance and dedication it will be difficult to pursue the kind of academic career that could give you the kind of financial security and brighter future you so much desire

Patience is a sign of maturity, In Isaiah 28:16 the Scriptures says; Therefore thus saith the Lord God, Behold, I lay in Zion for a foundation a stone, a tried stone, a precious corner stone, a sure foundation: he that believeth shall not make haste.

King Saul lost his throne, his crown, his precious relationship with God and ultimately his life through impatience *"Then he waited seven days, according to the time set by Samuel. But Samuel did not come to Gilgal; and the people were scattered from him. ⁹ So Saul said, "Bring a burnt offering and peace offerings here to me." And he offered the burnt offering. ¹⁰ Now it happened, as soon as he had finished presenting the burnt offering, that Samuel came; and Saul went out to meet him, that he might greet him. ¹¹ And Samuel said, "What have you done?" Saul said, "When I saw that the people were scattered from me, and that you did not come within the days appointed, and that the Philistines gathered together at Michmash, ¹² then I said, 'The Philistines will now come down on me at Gilgal, and I have not made supplication to the Lord.' Therefore I felt compelled, and offered a burnt offering."*

¹³ And Samuel said to Saul, "You have done foolishly. You have not kept the commandment of the Lord your God, which He commanded you. For now the Lord would have established your

kingdom over Israel forever. [14] *But now your kingdom shall not continue. The Lord has sought for Himself a man after His own heart, and the Lord has commanded him to be commander over His people, because you have not kept what the Lord commanded you."*
(1 Samuel: 8-15)

God has designed maturity to be a slow process

Jesus said in Luke 21:19; "By your patience possess your souls" Many has unfortunately lost their souls through their impatience.

Many results to taking short cuts when their plans doesn't seems materialized immediately, when their prayers seems unanswered according to their own fixed period, when the benefits of their businesses, education or investments seems unyielding, when their ministry doesn't grow as expected and we come up with a very popular sayings that heaven helps those who help themselves, if you know you can help yourself, why did you need the help of heaven in the first place?

The Scripture further says in Hebrew 12:1 to;

". . . **run with patience** the race that is set before us"

Even in the Spirit realm, we still have to be patient:

*"Better is the end of a thing than the beginning thereof: and the **patient in spirit** is better than the proud in spirit.*
(Ecclesiastes 7; 8).

Every foundation that needs to be built and maintained in your life requires patience.

Impatience could cost you your home, your future, your faith in Christ, your salvation and your life.

It takes patient to lay a solid and lasting foundation.

The wise man, who built his house on rock, was building a house with security and durability as his goal and the foolish man who built his house on the sand was building a house for show, their difference is fundamentally rooted in the type of visions they had.

The second man was not concerned about how long the house would be there. He just wanted to make sure for however long it was there, people would want to pass by and look at it and shower praises on him while the first man was building a house not only for beauty, but for security.

The two men experienced different results

The greatest contrast of everything is the results, because it says one house stood and another house fell. Not only did it fall, *"it fell greatly."* It was a total collapse.

What does the Lord want us to learn?

What is his fundamental point?

You have to notice something in the text. If you were to drive by both men's homes, you would not discover there was a difference. If you were to talk to the men, you would most likely not be able to notice the fundamental difference between the two.

The only time you would discover that there was a difference between these two men and their lives, homes, or ministries they erected, was during the storm.

Without wars, and trials you wouldn't have known the nature of foundations of David and Saul, only the storm reveals the true nature of your foundation.

As long as the weather is stable and the sun is shining, you won't think about what you're built on, you may not even care about what you're built on, but the storm has a way of letting you know what kind of foundation you're resting on. Notice the language. In both cases "rain descended," "floods came," "winds blew, and fell against that house."

Whenever you have rain, floods, winds, and houses being knocked down, that's a real storm, Stormy season came on both of them.

I wish the Christian life was really problem free like the way some televangelists portrays it to be — declaring that with Christ in your life, your stormy days are over, you'll experience no more pain, no sorrow, when you come to Jesus, he has keys of multiple blessings waiting for you, new home by the sea side, new infinity jeep; come to Jesus and in the next few months, you'll become a millionaire, come to Jesus, and he's got the healing for your every disease.

You can move a lot of people with that kind of sermon. But according to this text there was a real storm. Nature was unleashed, and rain and winds blew.

Our foundation must be formed before the storms come

It is safer for you to lay your foundation before the storm than to lay it during the storm, because it won't hold, this will lead to waste of materials and purpose will be defeated.

This is what you need to understand about foundations. Foundations can't be poured when it's raining. You can pour a foundation before it rains. You can pour a foundation after the rain. But you cannot pour a foundation when it is still raining. Whatever foundation you're going to have, you need to get it solidified before the storm comes, so when the storm comes you will not be in trouble.

Remember that foundation is not laid to repair a broken structure, but foundations are laid to solidify, to carry, to unite and to prevent the fall of an existing structure.

Storms have a way of causing you to forget the truth of God. Jesus has taught the disciple much about faith before they experienced the storm, yet, when the storm comes, they seem to have forgotten all he has taught them. They were sore afraid and thought the Lord cares less for them.

He has also told them of His coming death and his resurrection on the third day yet they were not expecting His resurrection and after the resurrection some of them still find it difficult to believe He has truly risen.

Storms have a way of causing you to forget what the Lord has said in His word. Storms also have a way of keeping you from applying in a storm what you have learnt in the sunshine. Their problem was not hearing the truth. The problem was applying the truth in a bad situation.

Why does God allow a storm in your life? Because it lets you know what kind of foundation you're on. Only in a storm will you discover whether you're really resting on the truth of God or whether you're merely listening to it. There's a lot of difference between saying amen on Sunday and saying amen on Monday in a storm. I have been to a country where our Sunday worship is always under a heavy military protection because of the terrorists. There I come to appreciate the wonderful freedom of worship that we enjoy in the western world. There's a lot of difference in worshiping God when all is well and worshiping God when all is wrong. But if your foundation is sure, then it will be the application, and not merely the information, of divine truth that will hold you steady.

The goal of biblical preaching is not merely to inform the body of the menu of the truth of God's Word. It is to bring them to the place of partaking of the meal. It is not merely to tell people, thus sayeth the Lord. It is not merely to explain to them what the Lord has said. It is to bring them to a change of action based on the truth of God. In other words, every time you have a storm, God has given you a new opportunity to demonstrate you are resting on a sure foundation.

CHAPTER—10

The Contrast between Elisha and Gehazi

We can picture Elisha and Gehazi in the Lord's story, they both represent, the two builders, they received the same instruction; experienced the same miracles, grew up in the same environment, but with different visions.

Elisha built on a good foundation and Gehazi on bad foundations. Elisha decided to serve God through Elijah, despite the fact that the road has not been easy, yet, Elisha endured, he chose to take the pain and build on the rock in his ministerial career because, he had a clear vision to serve God, and he was ready to deny himself, he was not looking for the present gain which perishes but eternal gain which endures forever,

The Scripture says in 2 Corinthians 4:18 "while we do not look at the things which are seen, but at the things which are not seen. For the things which are seen are temporary, but the things which are not seen are eternal."

Elisha endures the pain of building a solid foundation, even though it took him to withstand the insult of the sons of the prophet, yet he persevered, though it took him the pain of climbing the mountain with the master, yet he endured, though it took him the pain of crossing the Jordan with the master, yet he did, he paid the price to receive the double portion of his master's anointing, there is no short cut to glory. He endured the pain to receive the blessing, and he ended up as one of the greatest prophet the world has ever known, his ministry was built on integrity, righteousness and longsuffering. He received the double portion of Elijah's anointing that is inexhaustible, God wrought so many miracles through him, he became the spiritual backbone to the Israelites army, that even the king Joash referred to him as the Chariot of Israel and its horsemen (2 King 13:14)

God wrought the miracle of food through him in (2 King 4: 42-44) Shunamite woman received the miracle of child, (2 King 4:16-17) defeated the Syrian army to mention but a few, that even after his death, the anointing power on him still raised a dead soldier. (2 King 13:21) Of course, many people dreams of ministering in the power and spirit of Elisha, but how many people can really pay the price he paid.

If record is anything to follow, Gehazi ought to have received the double portion of Elisha's anointing, like Elisha, he also had a dynamic mentor, a great teacher and exemplary leader, the same way Elisha served Elijah, Gehazi also had the opportunity to study and serve Elisha, so if Elisha could get a double portion of Elijah's anointing, what portion of anointing would Gehazi had gotten from Elisha if he were to be a visionary? Double potion of Elisha's anointing means quadruple portion of Elijah's anointing!

A man of vision is a man with diverse possibilities

Gehazi was a good servant and a bad student, my heart goes out for him.

He served Elijah effectively as he could in the flesh, He was sensitive and very observant, for example, when Elijah, the man of God does not know what is missing in the life of the Shunamite woman or what she needed, it was Gehazi who discovers it, when Elisha asked *"What then is to be done for her?" And Gehazi answered, "Actually, she has no son, and her husband is old. (2 King 4:14)*

Gehazi witnessed all the miracles that God wrought through Elisha and also testified of it as well. "Then the king talked with Gehazi, the servant of the man of God, saying, Tell me, please, all the great things Elisha has done.

Now it happened, **as he was telling the king how he had restored the dead to life**, that there was the woman whose son he had restored to life, appealing to the king for her house and for her land. And Gehazi said, "My lord, O king, this is the woman, and this is her son whom Elisha restored to life."

(2 King 8: 4-5)

In spite of all these, Gehazi ended his ministry as a leper!

He built on a wrong foundation.

A man without a vision is a fearful man
(2 King 6: 13-17)

So he said, "Go and see where he is, that I may send and get him. And it was told him, saying, *"Surely he is in Dothan. Therefore he sent horses and chariots and a great army there, and they came by night and surrounded the city. And when the servant of the man of God arose early and went out, there was an army, surrounding the city with horses and chariots. And his servant said to him, "Alas, my master! What shall we do? So he answered, "Do not fear; for those who are with us are more than those who are with them. And Elisha prayed, and said, "LORD, I pray, open his eyes that he may see." Then the LORD opened the eyes of the young man, and he saw. And behold, the mountain was full of horses and chariots of fire all around Elisha. Because he had no godly vision, he was led by* sight, a man of the flesh. He acted in fear when they were faced with Syrian army

(Vs 17)

He was spiritually blind; a man without vision is a blind man. Alas! My master what shall we do, he was fearful and has lost initiatives. *"For God hath not given us the spirit of fear; but of power, and of love, and of a sound mind"*.

(2 Timothy 1; 7)

A man without a vision is a faithless man
(2 King 4:29-31)

Then he said to Gehazi, *"Get yourself ready, and take my staff in your hand, and be on your way. If you meet anyone, do not greet him; and if anyone greets you, do not answer him; but lay my staff on the face of the child. And the mother of the child said, As the LORD lives, and as your soul lives, I will not leave you." So he arose and followed her. Now Gehazi went on ahead of them, and laid the staff on the face of the child; but there was neither voice nor hearing. Therefore he went back to meet him, and told him, saying, the child has not awakened."*

Godly vision gives you confidence in God, His work, in His people and every situation.

Though Gehazi stayed and witnessed the miracles of God wrought through Elisha, yet, due to his lack of vision, his ability to perceive and trust God was being hindered

Though, he carried the staff of Elisha, his faith does not match what he carried.

Today, many travel around the globe looking for anointing end up in frustration because they lack the faith and passion to demonstrate it.

Here is a strong weapon lying waste in the hand of a sluggard, the same way the Bible lays waste in the hand of many a Christian!

Though he was sent on a mission, he lacks the faith to back it up

Hence, the staff of Elisha is useless and ineffective without his faith

A man without vision is a carnal man

"So he went down and dipped seven times in the Jordan, according to the saying of the man of God; and his flesh was restored like the flesh of a little child, and he was clean. And he returned to the man of God, he and all his aides, and came and stood before him; and he said, "Indeed, now I know that there is no God in all the earth, except in Israel; now therefore, please take a gift from your servant." But he said, "As the LORD lives, before whom I stand, I will receive nothing." And he urged him to take it, but he refused. So Naaman said, "Then, if not, please let your servant be given two mule-loads of earth; for your servant will no longer offer either burnt offering or sacrifice to other gods, but to the LORD. [18] Yet in this thing may the LORD pardon your servant: when my master goes into the temple of Rimmon to worship there, and he leans on my hand, and I bow down in the temple of Rimmon—when I bow down in the temple of Rimmon, may the

LORD please pardon your servant in this thing." Then he said to him, "Go in peace." So he departed from him a short distance.
(2 King 5: 14-28)

God used Elisha to heal Naaman, the Syrian captain of the incurable disease of leprosy that he had for many years Naaman was completely healed, and he could not have been happier with the results of his visit to Israel. It is easy to see why he would wish to meet with Elisha, and why he would gladly leave all that he had brought with him to pay for his healing. He urged Elisha to take it, but Elisha firmly refused. This was a work of God's grace, and he did not want Naaman to have any confusion at this point. Elisha did not want to leave room for Naaman to conclude that he had contributed, in some measure, to his healing. He also refused his offering in order to give all glory to God and to teach the gentile Captain of the unconditional love of God and to humble him that his healing cannot be bought with money.

It was only after it became clear that Elisha would not be persuaded to take any gift that Naaman asked if he could take some Israelite soil back to Syria because he was still limited by his pagan roots to a localized concept of God and thought the Lord could be worshiped only on the soil of Israel. As Naaman left to return to his homeland, it was apparent that he had gained much and had lost nothing but his arrogance and his leprosy.

Gehazi's Greed

He seems to have stood there, looking at all that gold and silver that was going back to Syria. To him, somehow, it seemed terribly wrong. I fear that there was a Judas-like spirit in Gehazi. The money, which meant nothing to Elisha, meant a great deal to Gehazi. And think of how Gehazi could have rationalized taking the money. Like Judas, he could have argued that these were difficult days, with famines and economic hard times. That money could have been used to feed the poor. This would overlook the fact that the poor had been fed anyway, without the use of "foreign funds.

"But Gehazi, the servant of Elisha the man of God, said, "Look, my master has spared Naaman this Syrian, while not receiving from his hands what he brought; but as the LORD lives, I will run after him and take something from him." [21] So Gehazi pursued Naaman. When Naaman saw him running after him, he got down from the chariot to meet him, and said, Is all well? And he said, "All is well. My master has sent me, saying, 'Indeed, just now two young men of the sons of the prophets have come to me from the mountains of Ephraim. Please give them a talent of silver and two changes of garments.'" So Naaman said, "please, take two talents." And he urged him, and bound two talents of silver in two bags, with two changes of garments, and handed them to two of his servants; and they carried them on ahead of him.

When he came to the citadel, he took them from their hand, and stored them away in the house; then he let the men go, and they departed. Now he went in and stood before his master. Elisha said to him, "Where did you go, Gehazi?" And he said, "Your servant did not go anywhere." Then he said to him, "Did not my heart go with you when the man turned back from his chariot to meet you? Is it time to receive money and to receive clothing, olive groves and vineyards, sheep and oxen, male and female servants? Therefore the leprosy of Naaman shall cling to you and your descendants forever." And he went out from his presence leprous, as white as snow.

(2 King 5: 20-27)

Note the resolve of Gehazi: "As certainly as the LORD lives, **I will run after him and accept something from him**"

(2 King 5: 20).NKJV

This was a very purposeful act on Gehazi's part. Gehazi's words are strikingly similar to Elisha's words in verse 16: *"As certainly as the LORD lives (whom I serve), I will take nothing from you."* Is Elisha determined not to take any gift from Naaman? Gehazi is just as determined to do so.

Gehazi was a waste to his generation, his lack of vision, has denied generations after him (until the day of Pentecost) the benefits of experiencing the power of God in greater dimension

His lack of vision has put an end to the power-shift of anointing that flows from Elijah to Elisha and that would have ultimately continue through Elisha to Gehazi and to generations to come but through his greed and lack of vision, he failed to maintain a right spiritual Foundation and his failure eventually put an end to his promising future.

He collected a reward for the miracle God himself has wrought, commercialize the gospel as some ministers of the gospel does today, some will not pray for people unless they pay for it, forgetting the fact that what they have is given to them by God and what they are giving out is received from God, we are just a representing hand of God to touch His people or is it not the gift of the Spirit the Bible calls it, then why should one lord over it. Has the Scripture not said "Buy the truth and sell it not?

(Proverb23: 23).

He collected a reward from the gentile thereby robbing God of His glory and Prophet Elisha of his dignity.

Consequently, he lost God's blessings as a result of greed and selfishness. He missed God's plan for him, lost God's purposes, God's abundant blessings and possibilities of quadruple portion of Elijah's anointing.

Contrary to his master's order, he lied, forsaking the priceless anointing and opportunity of immeasurable power shift. Instead of double portion of anointing, he inherited double portion of leprosy.

Many Ministers, whose god is their belly, are laying a wrong foundation today by following the footstep of Gehazi; they lack the vision, lost God's power through their greed and crippled their mission. The moment they are able to preach a little, speak a few tongues, quote some bible passages and wrestle with a few demons, they think they have arrived.

They lack godly visions and direction of purpose, they have forgotten that not all that glitters is gold, and they forsake the spiritual and go after material blessings, and ultimately perish for lack of vision.

Many people, who would have become great Man or woman of God, whose names would have been written in God's hall of fame have exchanged their glory for money like Gehazi, they were too greedy and ambitious.

Every Christian should respect their spiritual and civil authority for there is no authority except from God . . . (Romans 13 :1-4).

Therefore you must be subject not only for wrath but for conscience sake. Note — after David has cut the robe of King Saul, his tender conscience troubles him.

CHAPTER—11

Family In Crises

Because of the depreciating standard of family values, there has been an increase in domestic crimes in such an alarming rate such as the world has never known.

Spain is one of the most beautiful countries to live in, in the whole world, the country is beautiful, the weather is nice and the people are warm, accommodating and very lovely.

But they have a big family crisis, like cancer eating deep into the family life, destroying homes and every good thing the family stands for.

I have watched news on the national television of an eyewitness testifying to one of the most brutal killing of a woman by her husband. The witnesses at the scene recounted how the husband knocked his wife down with his car and ran over her, not once, but over and over and over until her lifeless body was badly mutilated.

Another man of almost 70 years old, putting a tyre over the neck of his 68 years old wife and set her on fire, watching and listening to her agonizing cries until she died. This followed a series of physical abuse unleashed on the woman over a prolonged period. The police had given him an order to keep away from the woman, but he breached the order and eventually killed her. Another man butchered his wife, cut her in pieces put her remains in a sack and tied her under the bridge, another not so far from where I live, killed his wife, the mother in-law, children and latter shot and killed himself. These are just to mention but a few of an unspeakable domestic violence taken place in our community.

The government in an effort to combat the domestic violence or 'gender violence', as it's been called over here, have implemented lots of preventive methods, increased security and amended the constitution in order to protect the victims of such crimes, but all these had very little or no effect.

The government eventually became part of the problem they intended to solve, they legalized same sex marriages, they also passed a law that allows girls as young as 16 years of age to have an abortion without parental knowledge or consent, and any interference or objection from the parents is considered a violation of the girl's civil rights, which is a punishable offence under the new law.

The role of the Church in this family declension

Some years ago, I attended one of the state's pastor's meetings in my area, and to my utmost surprise, one of the local pastors who had just written a book was given a chance to advertise or promote his book in the meeting.

The man stood up and began to address the pastors by saying that the importance of this book is to enlighten the pastors about the need of not forbidding teenagers of 16 years of age, who really love each other, to engage in sexual activities if they both consent, as long as they would like to marry each other in the future.

Can you imagine my amazement at what he said? I was enraged by his comments, one who claimed he was an evangelical pastor, yet he was advocating a pre-marital sex, totally ignoring Christ's teaching on this subject. Jesus spoke to seven churches in Revelation chapters 2 and 3, He highlighted the areas they were in breach of His doctrine, and, having identified their error, Jesus guides the churches peddling false doctrines and living in immorality to repent, or, suffer the most serious consequences possible.

The worst aspect of what happened was the blatant public acceptance by a man claiming to be a minister of Jesus Christ, of the open and public approval of a doctrine of Satan, note where the devil had chosen to sow his seed!

This was not being done in secret, as one may have expected, but publicly seeking acceptance of such behaviour, declaring the fact that the immoralities which Jesus warned about coming into His church was now acceptable today, clearly this false teaching was and is found in the hearts of some so called pastors today.

I was moved to speak but unfortunately, they said, there is no more time. That was the last time I attended such a meeting.

The government, the community and the worst of all, the churches seem to be ignoring the foundational values of family life let alone the very teachings of 'The Christ', thereby killing the future of the community and effective Christian fellowship.

The root of the problem is the problem of the root.

If the foundation of marriage is laid wrongly, the marriage will no longer be able to stand the test of time.

CHAPTER—12

Foundation Of Marriage

MARRIAGE WAS DESIGNED FOR SEPARATION IN ORDER TO CLEAVE

"Therefore shall a man LEAVE his father and his mother, and shall cleave unto his wife and they shall be one flesh"
(Gen. 2:24)

Marriage begins with a SEPARATION: making a choice, laying your priorities, leaving all other relationships. The closest relationship outside marriage is specified here, implying that if it is necessary to leave your father and mother, then certainly all lesser ties must be broken, changed, or left behind.

Separating ourselves from our parents does not mean to abandon them; it does not mean to depart or make a permanent sway. The bonds of love with parents are lasting ones. However these ties must change in character so that the man's full commitment is now to his wife. And the wife's commitment is now to her husband. The Lord gave the man this commandment, although the principle applies to both husband and wife, because it is up to the man to establish a new household that he will be responsible for.

Separation is needed to enhance concentration and be focus on his new responsibility. He can no longer be dependent on his father and mother; he can no longer be under their authority, for now he assumes headship of his own family. The adult must continue to honour his parents and care for them when necessary and assume responsibility for them rather than responsibility to them.

(See Matt.15: 3-9 and 15: 4-8).

Giving your full and sincere commitment to each other as husband and wife means giving other things a lesser priority—your business, your career, your house, even your hobbies, your talents, your interests, or yes, even your church work.

Herman Abrahams wrote '*Unless you are willing to "leave"* everything else, you will never develop the beautiful oneness of relationship that God intended for you'

One cannot really cleave unless you LEAVE. This has been the problem of many people today because they are trying to cleave even though they are not leaving their parents, jobs, businesses, friends, hobbies etc., you are not being asked to abandon them, you just have to give them a lesser priority. It is also of no use leaving, unless you are ready to spend a lifetime CLEAVING.

A couple once approached me that one of them (the wife) while praying, God told her to be worshipping in a different Church and the husband to remain in our Church, I asked the husband if he has also prayed over this and he said yes, he has prayed and confirmed it, then I said on this junction, you have to follow your wife, but why pastor? I said my God is not author of confusion, you don't offend me and you are very useful in my ministry, but your family comes before the Church, God cannot ask you to be worshipping Him in two different places, I strongly believe in marriage as God's institution and whatever God has joined together, let no Church put asunder.

Whenever I am counselling the couples before their marriage, I always stress the importance of the fact that marriage is not meant to be endured but to be enjoyed, however, it is very unfortunate that many people endure their marriage instead of enjoying it and their wedding anniversary is just the celebration of endurance.

Yet, judging by the divorce rates in many countries, many have not learned how to avoid this. Everyone wants a good marriage, but few are willing to follow God's instructions that, if followed, would produce loving, enjoyable and committed relationships.

God designed marriage and wants us to be happily married (Genesis 2:24). For success in this area of life, we need to learn from the Creator of marriage the principles that lead to happy, successful unions. In short, we need to understand and apply concepts that work rather than following modern paths that so often lead to failure.

Dating or courtships: Passage way to the Alter

A lot of books have been written and series of seminars have been organized in order to help to make the troubled marriage work but unfortunately this seems not to have been making much difference and has not really been offering much help in preventing the alarming rate of divorce in our society.

The foundation for a good marriage is long laid before the wedding ceremony. Most problems encountered by various families today are due to the faulty choice of incompatible spouses.

The Scripture says in 2 Corinthians 6:14-16; *"Do not be unequally yoked together with unbelievers. For what fellowship has righteousness with lawlessness? And what communion has light with darkness? 15 And what accord has Christ with Belial? Or what part has a believer with an unbeliever? 16 And what agreement has the temple of God with idols? For you are the temple of the living God. As God has said: "I will dwell in them And walk among them I will be their God, And they shall be My people."*

When two mature people begin dating each other with focus on marriage, they must put a lot of things into consideration like: Does he believe in God? Does she obey God? What are his character and personality? What are this person's background and personal standards and values? What are his or her goals? What values does the other person hold? What are our similarities and differences? Are we compatible in any sense? What are his or her Preferences and dislikes; will this person be a complementary match? Can I love and respect him or her or vice versa. What is my strongest point of attraction to this person; if that particular aspect turns out to be defective or no longer there in the future, can I still love them? Often in modern dating, little thought is given to a potential partner for life — other than whether the two enjoy their sexual activity. Yet when two people refrain from the emotionally charged arena of sexual relations, as God instructs those who are not married, they can much more rationally consider the values and traits of a potential spouse.

As children mature in age and getting mixed up with their mates, they begin to ask their parents the question as to when they can begin dating otherwise known as going into relationship with focus on marriage. Even though, the Scripture did not give us any specific instruction as regards to when dating is appropriate, wise parents take up the responsibility of teaching their maturing children good Biblical principles that will help them follow God's standard conduct of behaviour, that will re-shape their lives, control their actions and guard them against any ungodly decisions that could make or mar their lives. Determining the readiness of the children to begin dating or go into courtship should be made by the parents, which is going to be based on their maturity and readiness to accept responsibility for their actions.

Pastoral counselling and prayer is also very vital to the success of any Christian marriage.

Before parents allow dating, they should teach and encourage their children to follow biblical standards rather than releasing them to do whatever comes naturally. It remains the parent's responsibility to teach them to embrace and respect Scriptural standards, as they are about to engage in dating. This may sound awkward to you but no responsible government also allows people to drive vehicles unless they are qualified.

In the absence of proper follow up, adequate instruction and guidance, many of these youths becomes promiscuous, often contracts sexually transmitted diseases, unwanted pregnancies and choosing wrong paths that seems enjoyable for the moment but which eventually ends up in anguish. There is a way that seems right to a man, but its end is the way of death. (Proverbs 14:12; 16:25) Without the proper instruction, many people will never experience happy marriage. Every caring parent has their roles to play in this very sensitive area in the life of their children, guiding them through comprehending God's standard of marriage is one of the greatest blessings children can receive from their parents and this will help them avoid living a life of intense unhappiness, regrets and wretchedness.

Praying constantly for them for God's guidance and directions right from their childhood, It is never too early to pray such prayers, we have to teach and grow them in our prayer, in guiding your children through such a very sensitive part of their lives, prayer should always be your first resource and not your last result.

Many adopt an idea in modern world that dating goes along with sexual intercourse in order to determine their compatibility. They also believe that sex is simply a natural expression of love between two people and thereby the natural thing to do for individuals "going together" in an exclusive dating relationship.

This practice is very common in Spain where I live, and all across Europe where immorality is legalized, over here its being encouraged, the relationship between you and your man or woman partner or pair as it's been called is recognized by the government just as they recognize a married couple, the family value has been brought to almost zero, so much that even one of the European president only reluctantly got married to his woman partner after he has been sworn in as the president of one of the leading European countries.

This same attitude is on the increase among many migrants in Europe, they move in to each other and begin to live together as husband and wife and even having and raising children out of wedlock, they themselves and even answer the title of husband and wife even though they have never been actually married in the registry or at the altar! (The Church) They are building on bad foundations, living in fornication and missing the sacred blessings of God. *"Marriage is honourable among all, and the bed undefiled; but fornicators and adulterers God will judge."*

(Hebrews 13:4).

When you ask some people about the spiritual stand of the person they are proposing to marry, they will say 'Just be praying for us pastor, he is religious, he does go to Church occasionally, they will even quote the Scripture to justify their actions, something like the Scripture says *"For how do you know, O wife, whether you will save your husband? Or how do you know, O husband, whether you will save your wife?*

(1 Corinthians 7: 16).

Pastor with the kind of dreams I am having lately, I know he will be saved. You are foolishly mortgaging your future and building your life and that of your children's future on probabilities? For Paul did not give you the whole assurance that you will save your spouse, he said, "Whether you will safe".

And the scripture quoted is not being rightly applied, the Bible did not say that you should marry an unbeliever, the scripture here is addressing the couple who are already married and one of them eventually get saved, that he or she should not leave the other because, through her good witness, he or she can win his or her spouse for Christ.

Sometimes ago, I met this man who told me of his intention to marry a particular woman with the past record of drug and alcohol abuse but as at this time she was clean, seemingly free of alcohol and drug abuse, but she still smoke heavily, he wanted to influence her but she ended up influencing him, within a short time, he started smoking secretly, and after a while, they decided to tie the knot (to get married). I called this man and warned him, but he told me that I should just be praying for them, and the other time he told me that God has just spoken to him (giving him the go ahead).

They travelled back to their country over there in Western Europe; because they know I will not conduct such wedding, they got married in the city hall registry and that marriage happens to be the shortest marriage I have ever seen! They went on the honey moon just immediately after the wedding and on the third day, the marriage died and the husband came home alone and has not set his eyes on the woman ever since, it should be well over12 years now! They built on a very bad foundation.

As two people consider getting engaged to be married, if they are wise they will seek premarital counselling.

Today, all around us, families are dropping like flies. They're falling apart faster than we can put them together. Why are so many marriages crumbling? Many marriages crumble because they are built on the wrong foundation. It doesn't matter how much money you put into it, it's not going to last unless it is built on the right foundation

CHAPTER—13

Antidotes For A Successful Marriage

ENTRUST YOUR MARRIAGE INTO THE HAND OF GOD

Marriage is not a man's idea but God's institution, when we respect and honour it, we shall be blessed by it, and when we undermined it, we shall surely suffer the consequence.

Like every other area in our lives, God is the pillar that holds our marriage, when, He is the chief pilot, and when absolute control is given to Him, He drives us to the land of our possessions where we derives peace, love, joy and fulfilments. Sometimes we might be driven through the rocky path, sometimes through the desert and some other time through the bitter water, as long as we allow God to be the captain of our marriage, He will make every crooked path straight, He will bring water from the rock and He will sweeten all bitter water of our lives. He will turn our Marah to Elim.

(Exodus 15: 23-27)

Prayer and Guidance from the Holy Spirit

Commit your ways unto the Lord and your thoughts shall be established
(Proverb 16:3)

"Man ought always to pray and not to lose heart", (Luke 18:1) in other words not to be fearful, not to complain, not to murmur, lament or be discouraged.

Prayer should be every family's first resource and not their last result, for the family that prays together, stays together.

The context and the foundation for success in family life is, as was true for marriage, the Spirit-filled/controlled life that gives spiritual wisdom which is essential for both parents and children in the home. The presence of the Holy Spirit is none other than the presence of the risen Christ, who is to be the head of every Christian home. We should and must practice love, forgiveness, kindness and patience. None of these is easy to practice and maintain without the help of the Holy Spirit through prayer.

We are definitely going to experience turbulence and various challenges in this very long marital and parenting journey. Prayer is highly needed to receive the power of grace to carry on.

When Isaac got married to Rebekah, he must have bought baby crib, stroller, shoal, baby towels, decorate and equip the baby room, in anticipation of their first child, he never knew that the baby that he was expecting in nine months will take 20 years to come.

This experience allowed Isaac to grow spiritually, maturing in his faith and such drew him to his knees in prayer to God asking for God to open the womb of his wife.

"Now Isaac pleaded with the Lord for his wife, because she was barren; and the Lord granted his plea, and Rebekah his wife conceived"
(Genesis 25:21).

This was a very challenging experience Isaac had to face, if you can identify with Isaac's situation, if you like Isaac, are waiting anxiously, seeking the face of God for a child yourself, be assured it is just a question of time, God Who sees also answers, as He answered Isaac's sincere petition will surely hear you also, when you seek an answer to your prayers and live a life in compliance to the doctrine of Jesus.

God said in the book of Isaiah 54: 1&21 *"Sing, O barren, thou that didst not bear; break forth into singing, and cry aloud, thou that didst not travail with child: for more are the children of the desolate that the children of the married wife, saith the Lord. 2 Enlarge the place of thy tent, and let them stretch forth the curtains of thine habitations: spare not, lengthen thy cords, and strengthen thy stakes;* Also in (Deuteronomy 10:14) *"Thou shalt be blessed above all people: there shall not be male or female barren among you, or among your cattle.*

(Isaiah 54: 1&2)

Everybody that had delays in child bearing in the Bible eventually gives birth to a child, however, it was always to a unique child, i.e., Isaac (Genesis 21:1-6), Jacob and Esau (Genesis 25:22-27), Joseph (Genesis 30:22-24), Samson (Judges 13:2-7,24,25), Samuel (1 Samuel 1:2:21), John the Baptist (Luke 1:57-60),

The key to every closed womb is in the hand of God, as God opened all the closed wombs in the Bible, He will open yours also, I declare today that the womb of every barren person reading this book be opened in Jesus name. Jesus said to him, "If you can believe, **all things are possible** to him who believes."

Nobody died without a child in the Bible except Michal, Saul's daughter, who, having watched David, who had collected the Ark from the house of Obed-edom to bring it up to Jerusalem, *"and David danced before the Lord with all his might and was only wearing a linen ephod. And as the ark of the Lord entered Jerusalem, the city of David, Michal Saul's daughter was watching through a window and saw king David leaping and dancing before the Lord; and she despised him in her heart.* The whole account can be read in *second Samuel* chapter 6 However, the following verses reveal that David held His Lord above that of his wife, which is exactly what Jesus taught.

Reading the following verses reveals David's heart; *"Then David returned to bless his household. And Michal the daughter of Saul came out to meet David, and said, How glorious was the king of Israel today, who uncovered himself today in the eyes of the handmaids of his servant, as one of the vile fellows shamelessly uncovereth himself! And David said unto Michal, It was before the Lord, which chose me before thy father, and before all his house, to appoint me ruler over the people of the Lord, over Israel: therefore will I play before the Lord.²²And I will yet be more vile than thus, and will be base in mine own sight: and of the maidservants which thou hast spoken of, of them shall I be had in honour.²³Therefore Michal the daughter of Saul had no child unto the day of her death*

(2 Samuel 6.21-23)

Isaac must have thought that the journey was going to be easier, being the son of the great prophet of the Most High who speaks to God face to face, a man God choses as His friend, with all the covenants God had with Him, what would have happened if Isaac had not sought His face in prayer. This is telling us something about prayer, that praying to God is not teaching or forcing God to bless us, but rather it is an expression of our acknowledgement of God's mighty power, and to build our confidence in Him, God was going to bless Isaac, but that blessing will not come until Isaac activates the covenant He had already established with his father through prayer, even though, we are the children of the ach-bishop, we still need to build and develop our own personal relationship with God.

When asked the secret of my marital success, my answer is "the grace of God and a good wife and mother." All honest spouses will admit that marriage is nothing we can do successfully by ourselves alone with our resources. The challenges that face families today can be met successfully only by our absolute dependence on the Holy Spirit, who gives us wisdom and grace far beyond ourselves.

*We have also the . . . **Church of God**

After the day of Pentecost, there was a need for the followers of Christ to dwell together in unity for His purpose to be accomplished. We need a time to minister to God and be ministered to. We need to strengthen our relationship with Him.

We need to grow in faith, for it is impossible to please God without faith, and faith comes by hearing, and hearing by the word of God

(Romans 10:17).

Even though you have the Bible to read, you're going to need some exposition, explanation, and teaching to really understand what the Lord is saying to you. For example, the Ethiopian Eunuch, "Then Philip ran up to the chariot and heard the man reading Isaiah the prophet. "Do you understand what you are reading?" Philip asked.

v31 *"How can I," he said, "unless someone explains it to me?" So he invited Philip to come up and sit with him"*
(Acts 8:30-31)

The Church is the most effective channel through which the Lord flows to reach the world and make His will know to them. *"So thou, O son of man, I have set thee a watchman unto the house of Israel; therefore thou shalt hear the word at my mouth, and warn them from me.*
(Ezekiel 33:7)

The Church is the body of Christ; if you neglect the Church are you not neglecting Christ? *"So we, being many, are one body in Christ, and every one members one of another".*
(Romans 12:5)

The Church is an active body, living, moving, supporting and encouraging each other; it is also a living vine, in which every member is united to its fellow with the possibility of fruitfulness.

The Church also is the body of Christ and this declares the in-escapable involvement of every member in its corporate life
(Ephesians 2: 19-22; 4:15-16)

The Church is the Family of God, where we have mutually interdependent relationships that give accountability and encouragement. Those of us who are in Christ realize we have kingdom relationships within the eternal family of faith that transcend even our earthly relationships, which is what Jesus taught (Mark 3:31-35). We are actually Jesus' brothers and sisters, in Christ we belong to one another with God as our heavenly Father.

This is a great word of hope for those whose families are fragmented :

The heavenly Father becomes a father to the fatherless (Psalm 68:5) and he is able to place the lonely in his spiritual family

"A father of the fatherless, a defender of widows,
Is God in His holy habitation
God sets the solitary in families;
He brings out those who are bound into prosperity;
But the rebellious dwell in a dry land. (Psalm 68:5-6).

This is a word of encouragement to single parents and also to children who have become estranged from or even disowned by parents who reject the message of Christ, those who are still nursing the wounds of separation and abandonment.

What does the successful Christian family find? They find hope, strength, encouragement, instruction and accountability in the Church family, through its worship, teaching, fellowship, ministry and discipline. It's in the context of the greater church family that we learn to live by the power of the Holy Spirit, to restore broken relationships through love, patience, faith and reconciliation and to submit to one another "out of reverence for Christ and surrender to the will of God."
(Ephesians 5:21).

Father's, as the spiritual leader in the home, are to lead their family to be a part of the Church and be regular in attendance and involvement (Hebrews 10:25). However, if the father neglects this God-assigned role, often the mother has to assume this role as spiritual leader, always with the hope that her husband will realize his place in Christ and take over this important role

CHAPTER—14

Child Rearing

To BEGIN WITH, what should be our fundamental approach to child rearing? The question now is, where can we find sure and reliable information to guide us in this crucial responsibility?

The answer is in the Bible. It has much to say about this all-important subject, and parents should search it for correction and guidance.

Our behaviour toward our children is maybe the single most important aspect in proper upbringing of our children.

Do we really love and care for our children?

Do our words and actions express our sincere love for them? Will we, and do we, sacrifice for them?

Do we make time to show that we really care for them?

There is no substitute for time spent with our children!

Our time is our life. To our children, our time with them is life. A parent who provides his children with plenty of material possessions but little personal time is missing a vital point (an excerpts From Making life Work), Children do not equate the parent's time on the job working to provide for the family with love for them.

How do they see it? They think it means Dad doesn't like to spend time with them. Our time is the most valuable gift we can give to our children, especially quality time interacting and conversing with them.

Our call as missionaries has taken us to many countries including, Jamaica, Panama, to mention but a few, as a result of these, our children also paid the high cost of missionary life because whenever we move, we move them also, out of their schools, their friends etc., and all this has not been easy on them. When we eventually moved to Spain, we still moved our bases for some time before we finally settled down, though, they are good, in fact, we believe they are very good children and a great blessing to us, but these moves really took a toll on them.

I learnt a great lesson lately when I travelled to take care of our newly planted branch of our church in Germany, I asked my son to come and stay with me for some time, during his stay, we had time to talk deeply and shared some very quality time together, just the two of us, it was the most precious time I ever had with him, the period was like eternity to me, It made a great impact on both of us. Then I discovered the importance of spending time with them because after all, they're not going to be with us forever.

Without a foundational approach of love, little that we can do in rearing our children will produce the favourable results we want to see: mature, responsible and caring young men and women.

Be parents to your children and not a friend, many advocate that being a friend is the best, but I tell you, the best is to be what God has call you to be, a father and mother respectively.

Remember, friend's only advice but they can't instruct their friends, they cannot train, can't direct, can't discipline and can't make provisions and shoulder responsibility to a certain extent.

(1 Chronicles 28: 9-10)

Words and actions

In child rearing our words and actions have lasting effects on the children. Sometimes, parents become frustrated with their children's bad behaviour. It is easy for a father or mother to bear the impression that he or she does not love the child. Some parents, by means of angry, frustrated reactions and comments, make their children feel they are worthless or despised by their parents.

Children spend seven to nine hours outside their homes on school days, they receive continuous instruction and teaching some of which might be against their faith and upbringing, and they also receive continuous influence, negative and positive, from their fellow students and friends. They spend a longer part of their lives outside homes and away from their parents, sometimes they are passing through a lot of difficult moments, some are being bullied and ostracized by their school mates, some will even hide it from their parents, not wanting to make them feel bad, thus pretending that all is well and the only thing they are looking forward to is getting back home to receive, love, comfort and encouragement from their understanding parents.

Some, however, do not return home to parents that are able to be sensitive to their needs to their feelings, instead, they even aggravate the situation by shouting, yelling instructions at them, yet, and very sadly, when a parent tells his child he's no good, he is just confirming what they call him outside, and of course, the child soon will start believing it and living up to that reputation.

To show active rather than passive love for our kids, we must extend sincere compliments and praise when they're due, be sensitive to their feelings and understand their pains. This reassures our children they are loved and appreciated.

Above all, the duty of every parent is to continuously intercede on his or her behalf. We should pray for the protection and growth of our children, and for our wisdom in lovingly teaching and correcting them. And when they leave the home and go off to university, or their first job, we pray for them to meet the right kind of people and for them to meet the spouse God wants them to marry

CHAPTER—15

Building On A Right Foundation

Jesus Christ, Our ultimate foundation
(1 Corinthians 3:11)

"For no other foundation can anyone lay than that which is laid, which is Jesus Christ."

The foundation speaks of the deepest part of our understanding of biblical truth. It indicates what we believe to be the base or the root. Our foundation is not what we have projected it to be. It is the actuality of our purposes. It shows what we believe to us as a lasting and eternal value. It is what we will live and fight for. It determines how and what we do with our time, life and resources. It serves also as the lens through which we understand the meaning of life.

We all have foundations. I believe that just few people have a conscious understanding of their foundation. I believe even few people are standing on the right foundation. Many believe and claim they have such-and-such a foundation, but actually, they do not. Many have been indoctrinated by another person's foundation—but they do not own it for themselves. Many have the right foundation label but it is erroneously channelled to the wrong path.

At this junction, I want you to take some time to examine your foundation. Take a shorter route across your statements of foundation and come to grips with your life foundation. What are your intentions? Why do you make the choices you have made? What is your hope or reasons for living the life God wants for you? Are you really standing on solid foundation?

Jesus Christ is the one and only true Foundation. 'He is here', 'He is alive'. 'He is with us'. Jesus alone continues to make us right with God.

He continuously makes intercession on our behalf, He is our helper, He is our comforter, He is the lens through which see, He is our advocate, and He alone holds the power to develop us into the people according to His purpose. He alone is our wisdom. Jesus alone chooses and controls the agenda of our lives.

Jesus alone chooses and controls the agenda of our lives as long as we let Him by living in obedience to His teaching, it is, however, certain, that He will not force Himself or His will on us, as He said "Behold I stand at the door and knock, if anyone hears my voice and opens the door, I will come in to him and dine with him and he with me"

(Revelation 3:20)

God chose the agenda for Adam and Eve in the garden of Eden, in Genesis 1:18; 2:26-28, but it is their responsibility to walk in obedience to God's teaching, also in the Book of Exodus, God chooses and controlled the agenda of the children of Israel from their exodus from

Egypt to the entry into the land of Canaan, meanwhile, as God leads them through Moses and latter on through Joshua. He made it very clear, anybody who does not want to walk according to the agenda, or rules He has laid down better depart now, an entire generation perished in the wilderness because they failed to live according to the teachings and principles laid down by God.

It is the same today for Christians, it is the responsibility of everybody to live and move according to the teaching of Jesus, Read Matthew Ch. 5,6 and7 and note, Paul, Peter, John and James all confirm the doctrine of Jesus applies today.

By reading the story of Exodus through to Joshua, you follow the children of Israel from the crossing of the red sea following the pillar of fire and following the ark on to crossing the Jordan's river many years later, it was each individual's responsibility to live and move according to God's agenda.

For the Christian today, this is exactly the same scenario, we live according to Christ's teaching, living and doing according to His agenda and not ours. God instructed them to create the city of refuge; *"then you shall appoint **cities** to be 'CITIES OF REFUGE' for you, that the manslayer who kills any person accidentally may flee there"*

(Numbers 37:11)

As it was in the Old Testament, so it is today, Jesus Christ is our city of refuge today, have you sought refuge in Christ?

Note, if the manslayer, back in those days, accidently or intentionally strayed too far away from the city of refuge, beyond the boundary point where he would receive the protection of the city and was killed by a member of the family whom the manslayer had killed, the one who had laid in wait and taken the opportunity and killed him was not guilty of murder but was in fact innocent. Why? Because the manslayer had not obeyed the rules, remaining within the area of protection, he strayed beyond the area of his protection and paid the price.

Our job, once we have been granted Christ's protection from judgement and condemnation is to abide under the protection of Jesus Christ. How? By trusting in Jesus Christ death on the Cross and resurrection from the dead, then live according to the rules of that gift of forgiveness and Christ's protection, not disregarding Christ's teachings He gave to those who accept the invitation and choose to 'deny self, take up their cross and follow Him.'

As Christians, we agree that Jesus chooses and controls our agenda, but it is also our responsibility to live according to that agenda, we have a choice to make, either to accept or reject the instructions given to us by the Lord on how we are suppose to live our lives when we follow Him.

The Christian's true foundation is squarely accessed in the life of another, however, A Christian does not operate, control or work his or her Foundation how they feel, but, according to what another has instructed, Jesus the true foundation works Himself out in us as we live according to His teaching, day by day.

"Jesus said, 'I am the way, and the truth, and the life; no one comes to the Father, but by Me.'" (John 14; 6). Jesus also said, 'Ask and it will be given, seek and you will find, knock and the door will be opened'. We are instructed to 'Ask' and if we do it will be given (in Greek ask here means to 'keep on asking') so, you ask and keep on asking and He will give you 'the way' this 'way', which is given in the

life of Jesus is found by asking, you will find that He will reveal that by living your life day by day as He did, He in obedience to His Father, will lead you to live your life in obedience to what Jesus asks you to do. Then He went on to say, 'seek and you will find' (again in the Greek, seek here means to keep on seeking).

As you seek and keep on seeking He will reveal the truth to you, the truth about how you are to live according to His teaching as He lived according to His Father's teachings, you will also discover the truth about who you are in Him when you live a life of obedience to His teaching, about the truth of who He is in you as you walk the path of obedience to His teachings. He is 'The Truth', that means, by walking in obedience, you will live a life and not be deceived by the later day deceptions, because He will always lead you in 'The Truth'.

Jesus concluded by saying 'I AM The Life' The Life is accessed by you knocking and the door will be opened, for if you knock and keep on knocking the door will be opened, for the Lord Himself is the Door to every blessings in heaven and on earth.

Jesus said, "I am the door, by me if any man enters in, he shall be saved, and shall go in and out, and find pastures"

(John 10:9)

So, if Jesus Christ becomes the Way we are to follow, He being our example. Jesus was single-minded in always putting His Father's will above all and every other demand, we, likewise, place what Jesus wants above all other demands on our life, what Jesus teaches, the teaching of Christ comes first, what He says we are to do, we are to do and all else comes after this.

Matthew chapter 5, 6 and 7 is where Jesus lays out clearly His doctrine, His teaching, He makes it clear, this you are required to know, and, obey! If you do so, you will never get lost, if your belief in Him as the Truth is real in your life, you will accept that His teaching is in fact 'The Truth' you and I are to follow and live by. By living this way you will never be deceived, and, if He's the path of life that you follow, you will live eternally with Him

It is only in Christ Jesus that we can find the comforting Holy Spirit and the lasting pastures where He leads. He is the ultimate door, which leads to eternal life.

The way you live must be in accordance to what He teaches, in doing so, having asked, and the clear way He want's you to live is revealed, having been seeking, you have discovered 'The Truth' about Him, who He is and what that means for you, so then you knock and keep on knocking, and He opens the door to life eternal for you.

Faith in Christ is not merely a life lived according to principles. It is a life dependent on the person of Christ, by trusting in Him you demonstrate this trust by doing what He said in Matthew 5, 6 and 7 for example. Jesus, through the power of the Holy Spirit, who is present to lead and empower His people to live their life according to His plans and purpose, the Holy Spirit works in His people and motivates the members of His body to be obedient to Christ's teachings.

Jesus said *"Abide in Me, and I in you. As the branch cannot bear fruit of itself, unless it abides in the vine, neither can you, unless you abide in Me."* (John 15:4) To 'Abide in Me', means to live your life in unity with Him, in relationship with Him, you want to know all he said, so you can find out all he wants you to do.

In Matthew Chapter 5, 6 and 7 there are clear things Jesus wants you to do and things He does not want you to do. Go and find out what they are and ask Him to empower you to live a life according to what He said.

Note, they say, 'you can't take it with you', whoever they are, and however, Jesus said you can, that's right; you can transfer your wealth from earth to heaven! So how do you do that? Well read Matthew chapter 5, 6 and 7 and you will find out.

Remember, some of the things Jesus teaches comes with clear rewards if you do them in accordance to how He says you are to do them. Find out what they are and do them.

I cannot over emphasize the significance of this Foundation. This life "in" Christ is the life of obedience to His teachings; this is the rock that we must build our personal lives on and the life of the Church.

The result of the self-effort driven life often leads to lack of interest, passion and concern in the Church. The life Jesus teaches is not a life of legalism that Paul in Galatians warns about. What Jesus wants is not a life based upon law, but, a life focused upon the person of Jesus, pleasing The Father, empowered by The Holy Spirit, walking in love, but in obedience to Christ's teachings, so keeping our garments clean.

By living a life of legalism we bear the fruit of pride and self-righteousness, where we think what we do makes us righteous, but this is a long way from the truth.

Christ has already made us righteous by giving this garment of righteousness as a gift, and purchased by His work on The Cross. He having been given this wonderful gift that is enough for us to gain access in to the presence of The Father in heaven is a truly valuable gift, our job is to accept the free gift and look after it, by respecting and loving the one who paid for the gift.

How do we do this? Simple! Read His Words then do what He said His followers would do. Don't take what He said with a pinch on salt, we are to listen attentively, we are to take on board what He said, then, we are to go on and live our lives in an act of worship and love by doing what He teaches. In doing what He asks, we show our love and respect, keeping clean and not soiling that which He paid so high a price to give us freely.

The best results of a life following Jesus come from a life of total dependence on Christ; this is achieved by making Him the focus of our attention. We become extremely grateful for the gift of life and acceptance that Jesus has purchased for us by His finished work on the Cross of Calvary. The Church, which is a body of believers and followers of the teachings of Jesus becomes a divine alter, where our humanity meets Christ's Divinity as we meet together in unity, the place where we are reminded to draw nearer to and rely upon Him.

Even while convicted of sins that defile, we learn to lay aside those things, which defile and replace them with those things which edify, we leave the fellowship after the service with our eyes fixed on Him. He is the source of the power we receive for a life of change and we feel secure in His love for us.

Apostle Paul was highly inspired by this foundation in Christ. Paul was a religious man who formerly used religion as a way to support his self-foundation, justify his acts and also to display his own strength. After meeting the Lord on the road to Damascus, his focused was completely changed. He now wanted to know the Lord in a real and personal way. His identity was no longer based on himself and his work, but on the person and work of Christ.

Paul identifies himself with the crucified Christ and the resurrected Saviour; he attributed all his life and the accomplishments to the power of Christ that lives in him. Paul later wrote that he gloried in his weakness because when he was weak his was dependent and when he was dependent then he experienced the strength of Christ. Paul wrote of his new foundation: *"I am crucified with Christ: nevertheless I live; yet not I, but Christ liveth in me: and the life which I now live in the flesh I live by the faith of the Son of God, who loved me, and gave himself for me."*

(Galatians 2:20)

This dependence on Christ is not just a supernatural experience. We are to be anchored in the truth of the word of God and to meditate on them constantly. It is the study of the scriptures that actually point us to important life in Christ. We need to make plans and we need to make choices. In the midst of our decisions and plans, we are listening, teachable and flexible. We then become aware that God is working among us.

The place of a Solid Relationship in Foundation

Jesus Christ is our solid, lasting and secured foundation.

"For through him we both have access by one Spirit unto the Father. Now therefore ye are no more strangers and foreigners, but fellow citizens with the saints, and of the household of God; And are built upon the foundation of the apostles and prophets, Jesus Christ

himself being the chief corner stone; In whom all the building fitly framed together groweth unto an holy temple in the Lord"
(Ephesians 2:18-21)

We are super structure according to Peter, built upon Jesus.

"Ye also, as lively stones, are built up a spiritual house, an holy priesthood, to offer up spiritual sacrifices, acceptable to God by Jesus Christ.⁶ Wherefore also it is contained in the scripture, Behold, I lay in Sion a chief corner stone, elect, precious: and he that believeth on him shall not be confounded."
(1 Peter 2:5-6)

Christians as the lively stone derives their breath from the Chief Corner stone, every stone connected to him comes alive and becomes a living stone.

When Jesus becomes the foundation of your life, he becomes the foundation of everything that is built on it and whatever belongs to the building belongs to the foundation, including everything that comes on or that is brought into the building.

So if your life is built on Him, if your faith is built on Him, if your confidence is built on Him, if your future is built on Him, He will affect and perfect all that concerns you, which will lead to your success, safety and security.

The Conditions of building on the right foundation

The size of the building must correspond with the foundation.

If the building is faulty, it cannot fit the size of the foundation.

It must be "fitly framed" Ephesians 2:20 — No corrosion, must not be slack, must be of the same material

As you don't build brick on a wooding frame, likewise you don't build unrighteousness on a righteous God

Don't build ungodliness on a holy God

Don't build unfaithfulness on a faithful God

Don't build hatred on the God of love

What is the relationship between the foundation and the building?

Remember, as a Christian, you are the living stone built upon the 'Chief Cornerstone', which is what Christ alone has laid, and because you derive your life from the 'Chief Cornerstone' who is immortal, you are now intended to be one who will live forever in Christ. First is what He has achieved and laid down in advance, without which, we would not be able to build upon. Next, and of essential importance and necessity, how you respond to what Jesus has laid. Your building on what He has laid and not on what He has not laid. This is our responsibility, to accept His finished work, this requires that you know what He has done, and why, and accept His truths, then, apply His teachings to the way you live, thus, you are building upon His foundation.

The position of the Cornerstone

A: The cornerstone stays inseparably with the building;

Jesus said ". . . *lo, I am with you always, even unto the end of the world.* Amen.

(Matthew 28:20)

B: The foundation supports the building.

If Christ is the Cornerstone of all that you do, He will support you all the way; He says *"I am the vine, ye are the branches: He that abideth in me, and I in him, the same bringeth forth much fruit: for without me ye can do nothing.*
(John 15:6, Matthew 11:28)

C: The foundation binds the building together

He is God of unity *"Now therefore ye are no more strangers and foreigners, but fellow citizens with the saints, and of the household of God; And are built upon the foundation of the apostles and prophets, Jesus Christ himself being the chief corner stone; In whom all the building fitly framed together groweth unto an holy temple in the Lord"*
(Ephesians 2:19-21)

D: The foundation sustains & bears the burden of the building

God will sustain and bear your burden, if you are connected to Him. "Casting all your care upon him; for he careth for you".
(1 Peter 5:7; Isaiah 9:6)

E: The foundation affects the lifestyle & influences the building;

When you and all that belongs to you are connected to Jesus, your entire lifestyle will be influenced and impacted positively through His divine anointing and will bring a complete transformation to your person and everything connected to you.

Even though, the foundation acts as catalyst to the building, nobody seems to take note of its great effects from outside unless the very building itself, which in returns, adorns, reflects, promotes and reveals the beauty and glory of the foundation

So, whenever the blessings of God come from the Cornerstone, the beauty will always be revealed in you, the Livingstone.

CHAPTER—16

Maintaining A Right Foundation

THE RELATIONSHIP BETWEEN the foundation and the building is vital to the existence, durability and well being of the building and this relationship can only be sustained if it well maintained.

Maintenance therefore will be our next focus as we explore the importance of our foundation. Since building on a right foundation is building a right relationship with God, every house built is in need of good maintenance for its continuous existence, security and durability.

Getting saved is not the most important thing but maintaining your salvation is, as the Scripture says *"Therefore, my beloved, as you have always obeyed, not as in my presence only, but now much more in my absence, work out your own salvation with fear and trembling; ¹³for it is God who works in you both to will and to do for His good pleasure"*

(Philippians 2:11-13)

I strongly believe that salvation is not a destination; it is a process, for the Bible says;

"Being confident of this very thing, that He who has begun a good work in you will complete it until the day of Jesus Christ" (Philippians 1:6)

The work, which is the work of our salvation, has begun in you but as yet not complete, does this really mean that when we got saved our salvation is not complete? Absolutely not, your salvation is in the finished work of Christ, though it is finished, everybody still has responsibility to keep that little baby born alive, healthy and growing through the feeding on the sincere milk of the word (1 Peter 2:2) and obeying it.

Getting healed or delivered also is not the most important thing, but remaining healed or delivered is. Many people have attended virtually every Church in their city, every miracle program, every revival services; they go from deliverance to deliverance, from pastors to pastors seeking prayer for the same thing and undergone repeated deliverance over the same problem.

Does that mean that all those men of God whom God has been using to pray for others that they receive their miracles and has been praying for you do not have same anointing to handle your special case? Absolutely not, it is high time for you to stop running and start listening, start building trust in God, who is your Saviour, Healer and Deliverer, your Pastor, the Shepherd over your soul, who is the visible representative of the invisible God. Your problems might be foundational. It is either you are impatient, for the word of God says, *"For ye have need of patience, that, after ye have done the will of God, ye might receive the promise"* (Hebrew 10:36) or, you have laid or built upon a wrong foundation, or you lack maintenance principle.

The Lord Jesus said "When an unclean spirit goes out of a man, he goes through dry places, seeking rest; and finding none, he says, '*I will return to my house from which I came.*'[25] And when he comes, he finds it swept and put in order. [26] Then he goes and takes with him seven other spirits more wicked than himself, and they enter and dwell there; and the last state of that man is worse than the first." (Luke 11:24-26)

If you don't follow the maintenance principle, it will be difficult for you to retain the foundational value.

Maintaining the relationship already established between our foundation and the building which is your family, your business, your job, your ministry etc. is vital to its success.

The question now is, how should I maintain the relationship between my family, business, job and Christ who is my Lord, my life and my foundation?

Whatever is built upon the foundation belongs to the foundation as Joshua said, as for me and my house, we shall serve the Lord (Joshua 24:15b) and Joshua is cognizant of the fact that everything that enters the building built upon this foundation becomes the foundation property and should therefore not be held from the foundation.

Many has been seeking the face of God for breakthrough regarding their businesses but when God eventually open that doors of success, and business booms, we suddenly becomes too busy to remember God, we soon forget His warning in Deuteronomy 8:10-18;

"*When thou hast eaten and art full, then thou shalt bless the LORD thy God for the good land which he hath given thee*".

[11] *Beware that thou forget not the LORD thy God, in not keeping his commandments, and his judgments, and his statutes, which I command thee this day:*

¹² Lest when thou hast eaten and art full, and hast built goodly houses, and dwelt therein;

¹³ And when thy herds and thy flocks multiply, and thy silver and thy gold is multiplied, and all that thou hast is multiplied;

¹⁴ Then thine heart be lifted up, and thou forget the LORD thy God, which brought thee forth out of the land of Egypt, from the house of bondage;

¹⁵ Who led thee through that great and terrible wilderness, wherein were fiery serpents, and scorpions, and drought, where there was no water; who brought thee forth water out of the rock of flint;

¹⁶ Who fed thee in the wilderness with manna, which thy fathers knew not, that he might humble thee, and that he might prove thee, to do thee good at thy latter end;

¹⁷ And thou say in thine heart, My power and the might of mine hand hath gotten me this wealth.

¹⁸ But thou shalt remember the LORD thy God: for it is he that giveth thee power to get wealth, that he may establish his covenant which he sware unto thy fathers, as it is this day"

We are too busy in our political positions, much work, tight schedules, a lot of meetings to attend, a lot of invitations to be honoured, and simply conclude, God understands.

You have replaced the position of the source of the blessing with the blessing, you have replaced the provider with the provisions, but you say God understands.

I use to work as a supervisor in a particular company, I enjoyed the work and was very much loved by the management, I was offered a managerial post in the company with the condition that I begin to work sometimes on Sundays, I was asked specifically to reconsider my religious activities, I rejected the proposal without giving it a second thought, soon afterward, after I prayed with my wife over my continuity in my place of work, It was very difficult as I don't have the guarantee of any monthly income from the church where I served as pastor, yet, I felt the Lord wanted me to take a step of faith, quit my job and start trusting Him to meet our needs.

It is always good to stand for God and maintain your relationship with Him at all cost because you will never regret it. Some years after I rejected the attractive post of a manager with the benefit of a permanent contract, which gives an assurance of financial security for the future, the company went bankrupt and was closed down, I am glad I took my stand and prefer maintaining a good the relationship with God to the temporary financial benefit of the moment, always take your chance on Him and you will never regret it.

We also use to have a business of internet café, call shop and Mini supermarket, the business was growing and doing pretty good until the time when the business begins get on our way and was about to affect our ministry as many customers prefer to make calls and browse on internet on Sundays and also on week days, whenever we are about to go to church that is when the customers begins to rush in to make calls as they complain that 'this is only time we have', since we have to work on the week days. We prayed and felt that a decision have to be made and that is to do away with anything that could hinder our relationship with God, we folded up the business and we are blessed for putting Him first.

Many have said that God knows I love Him; it's just that Sunday is the only day I have throughout the week to rest; you have forgotten how much you prayed for that job and you are allowing your job to be an obstacle to your relationship with Him and, Don't forget that "The blessing of the LORD, it maketh rich, and he addeth no sorrow with it"

(Proverb 10:22)

Many of you have fasted and prayed for husband, wife or to have a child and God has answered you but instead of enhancing your relationship with the foundation of your blessing who is Christ Jesus, you still come with old excuses of Adam to God, ". . . the woman you have given me . . ." Do not forget that the river that forgets its source will dry.

The principal key to maintaining a good foundation is 'Effective Communication'

What is communication? Communication is the imparting or interchange of thoughts, opinions, or information by speech, writing, or signs. Communication involves two parties

The Communicator and the Recipient (The transmitter and the recipient) From the definition, the communication is divided into 3 parts

The Verbal (speech), Written and Signs

1. Verbal Communication is the spoken word
2. Written communication is the written word
3. Signal Communication is communication by sign

God is the greatest communicator; He opens the door of communication to men. The world came into existence through communication; "And God said, Let there be light: and there was light"

(Genesis1: 3)

The whole of chapter one is full of God said, God call and God give orders also at the point of Adam's creation vs. 26,

"And God said, Let us make man in our image, after our likeness: and let them have dominion over the fish of the sea, and over the fowl of the air, and over the cattle, and over all the earth, and over every creeping thing that creepeth upon the earth.

God communicates first with man and asked Him to step into his inheritance

"And God blessed them, and God said unto them; Be fruitful, and multiply, and replenish the earth, and subdue it: and have dominion over the fish of the sea, and over the fowl of the air, and over every living thing that moveth upon the earth.

And God said, Behold, I have given you every herb bearing seed, which is upon the face of all the earth, and every tree, in the which is the fruit of a tree yielding seed; to you it shall be for meat.

And to every beast of the earth, and to every fowl of the air, and to everything that creepeth upon the earth, wherein there is life, I have given every green herb for meat: and it was so. (Genesis 1:2-30)

The Bible is God's written communication to us, where He communicates His will, His plan, His purpose, His intentions, His principles, His position, His authority, His majesty, His glory, His power, His love, etc

Jesus Christ is God's love communication to the World;

"For God so loved the world that he gave his only begotten Son, that whosoever believeth in him should not perish, but have everlasting life.

(John 3:16)

The Church of God is the communication centre, where He communicates His will, His promises, His intentions and His goodness to us and we, in return communicates back to Him in appreciation of His person and greatness of His majesty in worship, giving and obedience.

God also communicated His will to man. *"And the LORD God commanded the man, saying, of every tree of the garden thou mayest freely eat . . ."* (Genesis 3:16)

The world is created to communicate. Without an effective communication, there cannot be a perfect relationship. Prayer is communicating your needs to the Lord, the Lord said "ASK (or communicate with me and let me know), and it will be given to you . . ." (Matthew 7:7)

Worship is communication, the expression of His greatness, reverence, honour and adoration of His majesty.

Effective communication is the principal key to success in every relationship, without a good communication, the family crumbles, husband and wife needs an effective communication to maintain their relationship, the better the communication, the stronger the relationship.

Breakdown in communication is attributed to over 85% of divorce cases, it is either somebody is not talking or somebody is not listening or one did not actually understand the other

A good leader is a good communicator and

A good communication is saying what you mean

It was power of communication that destroys the tower of Babel. Strong communication was their stronghold, the secret of their success, and the lack of it was their detriment.

"And the whole earth was of one language, and of one speech. And it came to pass, as they journeyed from the east, that they

found a plain in the land of Shinar; and they dwelt there. And they said one to another, Go to, let us make brick, and burn them thoroughly. And they had brick for stone, and slime had they for morter. And they said, Go to, let us build us a city and a tower, whose top may reach unto heaven; and let us make us a name, lest we be scattered abroad upon the face of the whole earth.

⁵ And the LORD came down to see the city and the tower, which the children of men builded.

⁶ And the LORD said, Behold, the people is one, and they have all one language; and this they begin to do: and now nothing will be restrained from them, which they have imagined to do

(Genesis 11:1-6).

There is no evil in unity, in fact; God wants his children to dwell together in unity (Psalm 133: 1) there are different kinds of unity, there is unity of progress and there is unity of rebellion.

Their unity is that of rebellion against God and his purpose for mankind to "replenish the earth" for they said "lest we be scattered abroad upon the face of the whole earth.

This reveals the absolute power of communication:

"Go to, let Us go down, and there confound their language, that they may not understand one another's speech.

⁸ So the LORD scattered them abroad from thence upon the face of all the earth: and they left off to build the city.

*⁹ Therefore is the name of it called Babel; because the LORD did there **confound the language of all the earth**"*

Meaning, the communication broke down between them, which led to confusion and chaos and their motive was defeated ". . . and from thence did the LORD scattered them abroad upon the face of all the earth"

During one of our Sunday worship service in 1999, we received a Pastor and his family visiting us from the Czech Republic, he was desperate to discuss with me and I can boast of the grace God has given me to speak and understand four major language in Europe, but unfortunately, Czech is not part of them, I wanted to discuss with him also, so we have to discuss with the hand to manage a little communication, It is quite obvious that both of us are desperate to communicate and establish a relationship, all our efforts to communicate ended up in frustrations and for the first time, I appreciate the role of communication in building a relationship and concluded that even the deaf and dumb stands a better chance and communicate more effectively than the people who did not understand each other's language.

There Satan noticed the power and importance of communication, he also stepped in, God and the devil thereby communicates with mankind.

A breakdown in communication between the head of the government and the citizen, leads to confusions, loss of confidence, etc

CHAPTER—17

Re-Visiting Your Foundation

THERE IS ALWAYS a need for everybody to re-visit quite often the foundations of our lives, since in the foundation, consist the pillars, the walls, and most importantly the base on which everything stands.

Just as we visit the clinic regularly for checkups, just as we carry out regular inventories on our businesses etc. We need to pay attention to our foundations, when our once vibrant business begins to collapse, you are losing customers every day and you don't know why, you are working so hard and bring in very little, the solution to your problems may be to re-visit your foundation, are there any dishonest gains? Are you being unfaithful in the area of giving, most especially paying the tithe of your profit?

God says in Malachi 3:10

Bring all the tithes into the storehouse, That there may be food in My house, And try Me now in this," Says the Lord of hosts, "If I will not open for you the windows of heaven And pour out for you such blessing That there will not be room enough to receive it.

He also says in the book of Haggai; *⁴ "Is it time for you yourselves to dwell in your paneled houses, and this temple to lie in ruins?" ⁵ Now therefore, thus says the Lord of hosts: "Consider your ways! ⁶ "You have sown much, and bring in little; You eat, but do not have enough; You drink, but you are not filled with drink; You clothe yourselves, but no one is warm; And he who earns wages, Earns wages to put into a bag with holes." ⁷ Thus says the Lord of hosts: "Consider your ways! ⁸ Go up to the mountains and bring wood and build the temple, that I may take pleasure in it and be glorified," says the Lord.*

⁹ "You looked for much, but indeed it came to little; and when you brought it home, I blew it away. Why?" says the Lord of hosts. "Because of My house that is in ruins, while every one of you runs to his own house.¹⁰ Therefore the heavens above you withhold the dew, and the earth withholds its fruit.

(Haggai 1:4-10)

Is there any compromise of any kind? Are you idolizing your business, which is, putting it first before God?

Remember the bible says it is God who gives power to get wealth *"But thou shalt remember the LORD thy God: for it is He that giveth thee power to get wealth, that he may establish His covenant which he sware unto thy fathers, as it is this day"*

(Deuteronomy 8:17-19)

It is also worth paying a visit to the good starting point of your business, the changes you have made lately, the new products you have introduced, changes in the personnel, the staff you fired and the staff you employed, your expense before, during and after the changes, any financial commitments eating off your capital?

Is your marriage in trouble, before considering separation or divorce, have you re-visited your foundations? The need to re-visit your foundation is based on two applications. The first one is your spiritual foundation, where God is and still want to be your ultimate foundation. Take your family matter back to Bethel, the point of your first love, either of you might have shifted your focus from Christ, who is the foundation of your faith, remember, without Him, you can do nothing. God is definitely not going to force or impose Himself on you or on your marriage, but He is a concern father, because He loves love you and have a great plan for you and your family.

He said in Revelation 3:20 *"Behold, I stand at the door and knock. If anyone hears My voice and opens the door, I will come in to him and dine with him, and he with Me"*

For God to enter, you will have to open the door of your heart, commit your family and surrender your will to Him.

The second application is your marital foundation; probably as you are reading this book, you are saying, You don't have any idea what I have been through, and you don't know what it is to live with the kind of spouse that I have, you might be right, there is no question about that, but the main question is; what brought you people together in the first place, what are your points of attraction?

The problem with many marriages is that, a lot of energy is spent on focusing on your spouse's deficiencies than his or her merits.

The beauty of the marriage is not derived from the perfection of the couples but rather on their imperfections which is based on their desire to accept each other as they were with willingness to love each other in spite of their differences.

Life is full of challenges, but our challenges can be overcome by the power of love.

In marriage, everybody have a role to play, don't play the blaming game, because you are also a principal player and also contribute immensely to the success or failure of your marriage

If you can only concentrate on the merits of their spouses instead of their deficiencies, you will discover that you will find strength to forgive, love and move to ahead and his deficiencies will be turned to merit.

You may probably be thinking whether I am also a perfect man. To answer you, I am not, far from it! But I have a perfect marriage by the grace of God. I do not have a perfect wife also, but she is better than me.

Permit me to share this with you, you know women love birthdays and it is very important to them, they appreciate and love you more when you remember occasions that is very important to them, most especially their birthdays.

One day, I committed a great marital crime by forgetting my wife's birthday, normally, I do wake the children up very early in the morning to greet her and sing happy birthday and present the birthday gifts to her, but on this fateful day, I totally forgot, she woke up staring at me, not really expecting the gifts but at least the greetings, but I looked at her face and only greeted her with a "good morning", she looked me in the face and said "darling, today is my birthday", I felt so bad, I don't know what to do, I began to tell her how sorry I was and she just responded with a big smile rubbed her hand on my head and say, darling, you are getting old! We laughed over it and I promised to make it up to her.

She had every right to be angry with me of course, she has never forgotten any of my birthdays, she might have chosen to allow Satan to poison her heart with different kind of doubt about the insincerity of my love and different kind of things, though, she was faced with options, but she simply made a better choice to focus on my better part.

I have had to do the same thing also on several occasions, though we are twenty four years in marriage, but we have never stop talking about how we met for the first time on our way to evangelism outreach from our local church, how we were called back in the middle of the road and we were asked not to go out with our friends so that we will be able to concentrate on our evangelical mission.

However, in my case, I was blessedly paired with my future wife that day, we talked about it quite often and we laughed over it, but to our marriage, it serves as a booster to our relationship and energizer or fertilizer to our growing love because we constantly re-visit our marital Foundations.

Returning back to BETHEL, the place of our First Love

Maybe thirty years have passed since Jacob made his vow to God at Bethel *"Then Jacob made a vow, saying, "If God will be with me, and keep me in this way that I am going, and give me bread to eat and clothing to put on, so that I come back to my father's house in peace, then the Lord shall be my God. And this stone which I have set as a pillar shall be God's house, and of all that You give me I will surely give a tenth to You."*
(Genesis 28:20-22),

On Jacob's flight to Haran from Esau's anger, he has to stop overnight at a place called Luz. There, he gathers some stones for a pillow and goes to sleep; it was then the Lord begins to move in his heart.

There Jacob had a dream of a ladder that was set up on the earth to heaven and angels of God were ascending and descending on it.

And the Lord stood above it and proclaimed "*I am the Lord God of Abraham your father and the God of Isaac; the land on which you lie I will give to you and your descendants. [14] Also your descendants shall be as the dust of the earth; you shall spread abroad to the west and the east, to the north and the south; and in you and in your seed all the families of the earth shall be blessed. [15] Behold, I am with you and will keep you wherever you go, and will bring you back to this land; for I will not leave you until I have done what I have spoken to you.*"

[16] *Then Jacob awoke from his sleep and said, "Surely the Lord is in this place, and I did not know it."*

[17] *And he was afraid and said, "How awesome is this place! This is none other than the house of God, and this is the gate of heaven!"*

[18] *Then Jacob rose early in the morning, and took the stone that he had put at his head, set it up as a pillar, and poured oil on top of it. [19] And he called the name of that place Bethel; [a] but the name of that city had been Luz previously.*

[20] *Then Jacob made a vow, saying, "If God will be with me, and keep me in this way that I am going, and give me bread to eat and clothing to put on, [21] so that I come back to my father's house in peace, then the Lord shall be my God. [22] And this stone which I have set as a pillar shall be God's house, and of all that You give me I will surely give a tenth to You."*

(Genesis 28:13-25)

We wonder why Jacob did not come straight here to Bethel when he left the house of Laban, since it was in his heart to come back to Bethel in the first place. For whatever reason, Jacob has paid a price for not returning to Bethel. His detour to Shechem has cost him dearly. His daughter Dinah has been defiled and the conduct of his sons has brought reproach upon him in Canaan. What a lesson! We always pay a price when we sacrifice the eternal on the altar of the temporal. When we fail to keep our hearts in tune with God, our lives quickly fall into discord and disarray.

We all have decisions to make regarding our Foundations. Dr. M. Otabil said `Life can be so complex, depending on the choices we have made at the transitions of our life'.

You are who you are today because of the Choices you have made in the past, if you don't like your life, don't just pray over it, decide to make necessary changes. Many people are like Jacob today in that they have been to the place where they met God and have made a vow to Him that if he would help them with this or that they would live for him forever.

However, troubles, trials and gross sin have caused them to forget that vow. It is so easy to forget our vows to God after the storm has passed. Does that sound like you? Do you remember how, during that awful sickness, disappointment, or death of a loved one, when you lost your job, business, bankruptcy, you promised God to be faithful to Him? Have you kept your part of the agreement?

To us, Bethel represents the foundation of our faith, a right relationship with God. It was so in the life of Abraham, it was so in the life of Jacob, and so it is in our lives as well. Our Bethel is located in our hearts. This means that we can leave Bethel never once changing our geographic location and we can go back to re-visit our foundation, return to our Bethel at anytime and from anywhere!

"Then God said to Jacob, "Arise, go up to Bethel and dwell there; and make an altar there to God, who appeared to you when you fled from the face of Esau your brother."

(Genesis 35:1)

God had to call Jacob to go to Bethel. Had Jacob gone of his own accord he would have been spared much heartache and trouble. Why should we wail to return to our foundation, our "first love" of Christ when we have strayed from that love? Jacob was not as consecrated as he should have been. God called him back to the place of his first vision of God. Simple gratitude should prompt us to be in the right place, with the right people, on the right day, in the right way "unto the end"

(Romans 2:4; Jonah 14:15; John 15:14)!

As we learn from Jacob's return to his foundation, which is a point of right relationship with the God of Bethel, we can also make some important decisions that will change our lives forever.

It was approximately 30 years ago since Jacob had the Bethel experience. Later and Jacob's family was in a mess and he needed God. In verse 1 of our text *"God said unto Jacob, Arise, go up to Bethel, and dwell there: and make there an altar unto God, that appeared unto thee when thou fleddest from the face of Esau, thy brother."*

(Genesis 35:1)

Why is it that God has to remind him of the occurrence "when thou fleddest from the face of Esau, thy brother." that led him to his encounter with Him? Probably he has forgotten the occasion the moment his problem has been solved. God might as well be reminding some of us the vows we made to him on our way to the surgical theater, when we thought we had almost zero chances of walking out alive, when we are in financial mess and we don't know how our next bill is going to be paid, when we are facing a great family crises that's about to tear our family apart, when our business is on the verge of bankruptcy and we found out that we are not even credit worthy and we say Lord, if you see me through I will do this and that. Jacob was in the same situation, on his way from Harran, he went to Shechem instead of Bethel.

The Scriptures says

"Do not be rash with your mouth,
And let not your heart utter anything hastily before God.
For God is in heaven, and you on earth;
Therefore let your words be few.
3 For a dream comes through much activity,
And a fool's voice is known by his many words.
4 When you make a vow to God, do not delay to pay it;
For He has no pleasure in fools.
Pay what you have vowed—
5 Better not to vow than to vow and not pay.
(Ecclesiastes 5:2-5)

C. S. Lewis said, "God whispers to us in our pleasure, and shouts in our pain." Do we hear the voice of God calling us back to Bethel? Are we going to ignore God until we find ourselves in trouble?

The journey back to Bethel begins when we are ready to deal with our sin and purify our hearts and lives. The call of God brought awareness. In verse two. "Then Jacob said unto his household, and to all that were with him, Put away the strange gods that are among you, and be clean, and change your garments." Immediately Jacob knows that he cannot return to Bethel in his present state.

There are certain things in his life and his family that should be put away! No one needs to tell him what they are and what to do with them! What did Jacob need to cleanse, change, and put away?

He need to put away idols, foreign gods brought in from the strange land, like teraphim, the one Rachel had stolen from her father Laban, and probably some other foreign gods of the Canaanites adopted in Shechem, in addition to this there are also foreign culture and practices that clearly opposes the ways of God.

An idol is clearly an object of excessive devotion. In Matthew 6:21, the Lord Jesus said, *"For where your treasure is, there will your heart be also."* Our treasures are the things for which we make time and room in our lives and the family of Jacob allows all this to make room in their lives, they were not only following a wrong direction but also drawing Jacob along. All this indicates that Jacob was raising an ungodly family which will definitely hinder the purpose of God in the life of Jacob.

These are the things that ultimately rule from the throne of our hearts! Treasures come in two ways, earthly or heavenly!

There were hindrances. Notice verse 4. *"And they gave unto Jacob all the strange gods which were in their hand, and all their earrings which were in their ears;."* What were these *"earrings?"* These were not just adornments; they were earrings, which were worn as amulets or charms. They were connected with idolatry. Earrings of various forms, sizes, and materials, were universally worn in the East, and were connected with incantation and idolatry. Some of those earrings, were used as talismans or amulets, which were objects engraved with figures supposed to possess occult powers, worn as charms.

These trees were remarkable for their longevity; therefore they served as a reminder to them and future generations. This oak became a consecrated tree, bearing testimony to their repentance and return to God.

Sometimes it is good for us to make a public act of repentance and rededication but also take note of this following statement "And Jacob hid them under the oak which was by Shechem" Why hiding and not destroy them?

The purpose of hiding a thing generally is to be able to retrieve them latter, God did not want us to hide any of our attitudes on our way to His house or His presence, He wants us to come just as we are, God want us to destroy them because a dead body should be buried and not hidden!

They also need to "change their garments". (Genesis 35:2): Changing of garments is also a symbolic act, an outward act indicating an inward change.

How many things do we allow in our lives that send a mixed or negative message to a lost world? How many things do we allow in our lives that actually war with our soul? How many times do we do things, wear things, without even once thinking about their influence, implications and identity?

Jesus said Matthew 5:16 *"Let your light so shine before men, that they may see your good works and glorify your Father in heaven"*. We are the light not only through the words of our mouths alone, but we are to shine as light also through what we do, where we go and what we wear etc.-

Because of the compromise of Jacob's household, nobody would have believed them that they are the people of God, because their actions completely contradicts their profession.

It seems to me that people today are dumbing down and dressing down, even when it comes to God and His house. God's standard and requirements according to the Scripture is clear, our God deserves our best. As a society, we have lost our respect and reverence for God as well as the house of God. We have created a lesser God in our heart, one who is created in our image and according to our own likeness, one who is less holy, and less demanding, one who is happy with our compromise and indifference to our attitudes, one who is pleased with the crumbs of our lives that we throw at Him.

What does Bethel means to you? The House of God, Bethel is a place of acquaintance. The place of first love, it is Jacobs spiritual foundation, the place of his first encounter with God Many of us today need to go back to that place where we first met the Lord. Bethel is the place where you can go back and find power, and purity and peace. It is the place where you can go back and fall in love with the Lord again

There are a lot of people today that know less about God than they did when they got saved. Is there a time in your life when you were closer to God than you are now? As believers in Jesus Christ, we all have a personal walk with God. This is something quite different from our corporate or Church affiliation or our relationship, and responsibility. It is possible to be much involved in Church service and activities, yet not have a close fellowship with Jesus Christ.

This is the difference between doing and being. In reality, Church service and activity can become a substitute for a personal walk with God. The Scripture says *"But he that lacketh these things is blind, and cannot see afar off, and hath forgotten that he was purged from his old sins.*

(II Peter 1:9)

When we go back to Bethel, we can be certain of God's presence and protection. In verse 5 "And they journeyed: and the terror of God was upon the cities that were round about them, and they did not pursue after the sons of Jacob."

Jacob was afraid of the consequences of his son's actions. He feared what the Canaanites would do to him as the news of the Shechem massacre spread. As it turned out, his fear pushed him in the right direction!

So many times, believers who have walked away from God fear their journey back and Fear pushes them towards the wrong direction. Why? They fear what others will say or do. They fear as to whether they will be able to maintain that place or position, and that they might backslide again.

It is quite interesting that instead of Jacob needing to be afraid of his neighbors; his neighbors became afraid of him. When he put away his idols, cleansed his heart, and went back to Bethel.

The Scriptures says *"When a man's ways please the Lord, He makes even his enemies to be at peace with him."*

(Proverb 16:7).

We ought to never fear man, but rather to fear God. Returning to the Lord brings boldness, assurances and confidence.

Bethel is a place of revival and restoration.

In verse 7 *"And he built there an altar, and called the place El Bethel: because there God appeared unto him, when he fled from the face of his brother."* Here we get a sense that something is restarted at Bethel. Jacob built an altar to God, now he comes back to fulfill his promises and pay his vow. How often do we need to get a new glimpse of God? How often do we need to renew our commitment to building and maintaining our alters and keeping our vows?

Bethel is a place of reconnecting with God's purpose.

In verse 9-13, the Lord restates His covenant promise with Jacob. He reminds him of his new name as well. *"And God appeared unto Jacob again, when he came out of Padanaram, and blessed him. And God said unto him, Thy name is Jacob: thy name shall not be called any more Jacob, but Israel shall be thy name: and he called his name Israel. And God said unto him, I am God Almighty: be fruitful and multiply; a nation and a company of nations shall be of thee, and kings shall come out of thy loins; And the land which I gave Abraham and Isaac, to thee I will give it, and to thy seed after thee will I give the land. And God went up from him in the place where he talked with him."*

While Abram fled to Egypt because of the famine in Canaan, he did not hear from God, but when came out of Egypt, God spoke again with him Genesis 13:14) also in Genesis 26:1-3, when Isaac obeyed the voice of God by staying in Gerar, God reaffirms his covenant with him, Here Jacob is reminded once again that the covenant promise is still in effect and he has a role to play in fleshing out that promise, If we are obedient to God by being where He wants us to be, He will reaffirm and fulfill His purposes in our lives.

A man once stood before God, his heart breaking from the pain and injustice in the world. "Dear God," he cried out, "look at all the suffering, the anguish and distress in your world. Why don't you send help?" God responded, "I did send help. I sent you." We need to remember that we are the sent ones, "among whom you also are the called of Jesus Christ" (Romans 1:6). Jesus is telling us today, "as my Father hath sent me, even so send I you." Going back to Bethel reminds us of this!

CHAPTER—18

Repairing The Broken Foundation

Mending The Broken Foundations — Is there any remedy to the broken foundations? When the foundation is broken or damaged, the constructor carries out an urgent repair by applying the system called UNDERPINNING.

What does it mean to underpin? Underpinning is the process of strengthening and stabilizing the foundation of an existing building or structure by building extra supports for the foundation from beneath i.e., to avoid damaging or weakening of the superstructure. To begin underpinning, you have to excavate, without a good excavation, underpinning can be very difficult or almost impossible.

As you can see, many ministry is in need of underpinning, many homes are in need of underpinning, many businesses also is in need of underpinning to strengthen their various foundations.

Many marriages are tired of back to back crises, marriages that were at the verge of total collapse and in urgent need of a kind of foundational support to stabilize the foundation of their marriage, every constant arguments weakens the pillar of any relationship and you are going to need a kind of underground support to strengthen you, keep you going and enjoy every blessed day of your marriage, for marriage is not to be endured but to be enjoyed.

For this underpinning to have effect in your life, you are going to need a kind of excavation, because the new supporting pillar will not hold on a mere dirt, it has to be well unearthed, and you are going to need a shovel of honesty to shovel out dishonesty, disappointments, betrayals, lack of commitment, cheating, disloyalties etc., no pillar of truth will stand on all these, it has to be unearthed out.

Our God is the God of dry bones, I declare over your business, over your family and over your ministry that your excavated dry bones begins to receive life in the name of Jesus. As you read this book today, I declare every shackle preventing you from reaching your full potentials for God be broken in Jesus name.

No matter how seemingly impossible your situations may be, our God specializes in impossible cases that seemingly defies human solutions.

Underpinning is also necessary whenever the builder wants to add additional story to the building, at every transitional points in your life, where you need to climb up to higher level, underpinning is necessary to strengthen your foundation.

Furthermore, underpinning is also necessary, where there is no base or foundation, commit your ways unto Him who is the Foundation of the foundations, and He shall direct your path. (Proverb 3:5).

Whenever we live a life in disobedience to Christ's teachings and experience God expressing His dissatisfaction, disappointment and disapproval to our actions or behaviours, we shouldn't speak like Eli, as he responded to God's message sent through the young Samuel, his response was "It is the Lord let Him do whatever He likes" Does that sound like you?

Eli showed a sign of bad leadership by being indifferent to God's rebuke, he was neither a disciplined father nor an exemplary leader to Samuel, He did not teach Samuel how to react when God pointed out his sin to him, he didn't teach him that when God reveals He is angry with us, our response should be to submissively show a sincere sense of humility, remorse and repentance.

Is the anger of God Definite?

Of course not, for it is written that "His mercy endures forever "In Numbers 14:11-12 *"Then the Lord said to Moses: "How long will these people reject Me? And how long will they not believe Me, with all the signs which I have performed among them? 12 I will strike them with the pestilence and disinherit them, and I will make of you a nation greater and mightier than they."* God was determine to destroy the children of Israel, He was quite angry and seems resolute, but it took a humble Moses to selflessly plead on behalf of the people, and God changed His mind.

I was born and brought up in the Islamic faith growing to become actively involved. At that time I did not know much about Christianity, however, Shortly after my salvation, a certain minister of God, blessed with a wonderful fast growing ministry, who happened to be one of the people that actually preached to me, called me one day and introduced me to a group of Bible scholars across the globe. They felt that the Bible had become old and needed updating to include the names of the great men of God of our day, those whom God had been using in our life time, the reason was so the upcoming generation would know about them.

At that time I was so new to 'The Faith' and not knowing much about the Scriptures, however, the little I did know guided me to boldly tell him "it is written," and therefore, Scripture should not be added to nor taken from, nothing should be removed or added to scripture, full stop! Seeing, at that time, I had little knowledge of scripture, he tried to take advantage of me by convincing me otherwise, so I went to seek counsel and was advised that I had said the right thing and should move away from such a man that wants to add to the scriptures, he went on to point out that, if their plans are of the Lord it shall stand, if not, their plot will be thwarted and their group would be disbanded.

As I was growing as a Christian, I recalled the incidence, and latter discovered what the enemy of our faith had been using this man and his group to do; to attack and try to destroy the precious scriptures on which The Christian faith is built.

The Scripture says; *"For no other foundation can anyone lay than that which is laid, which is Jesus Christ.*

(1Corinthians 3:11)

This man eventually cheated on his wife and fell into the sexual sin of adultery, and instead of repenting, went further and began abusing alcohol; his ministry went down hill and he himself backslid. I paid him a visit to encourage him, in my own little way, when I met him he was smoking heavily and drinking alcohol in excess, these are the kinds of things he used to preach against. Whilst trying to encourage him, I was stunned by his reply, he said he regretted ever leading so many people to Christ and if he could get in touch with those people, he would have loved to advise them otherwise.

As a new Christian having come from a different religion entirely, I felt so confused and dejected by his words, I spent time pondering on what he had said, but as I began to meditate on the words of Jesus, I was sustained by the grace of God and the assurance of my salvation, the reality of my conviction of the person of Christ, who He is, what He achieved on The Cross for me, who I am in Him, this motivated me to press on along the narrow way, I was utterly persuaded of the hope I have in Christ!

I further tried to seek help for him, however, I was told, all that I could do for him, was to keep on praying for him, which I have done.

It was quite obvious that his foundation of obedience to Christ's teaching and faith in the finished work that Jesus achieved by His death on The Cross and rising from the dead, had not been effectively laid in his own life, any foundation that may have been laid had been clearly destroyed by embracing and teaching a false doctrine of Christ.

Yet the question, almost thirty years later, still lingers in my mind, regarding the hopeful restoration of this man by the laying of the true foundation in his life, after he might have bow the knee and ask Jesus to forgive him and turns away from his false doctrine to the truth.

CHAPTER—19

If the foundations are destroyed, What can the righteous do?

I F I ASK you the description of your house, you would most likely tell me about the colour, the design, the location, the square footage, the size and the number of bedrooms. But you probably wouldn't tell me about the foundation. Perhaps you don't know anything about your foundation. Yet, it is the foundation of your house that makes all the difference.

Proverb 24:3 states, "*By wisdom a house is built, and by understanding it is established.*" This is true not only of your house; it is also true of your life.

Some years ago, we bought our first Church hall, when I saw the building, I was captivated by the appearance, the location and the seize, It appears to be all that I have been dreaming of, we started by renting it and when the owner comes with the offer to sell the place, we gladly jumped at it, looking for finance everywhere to buy this magnificent place which was eventually made possible by the grace of God.

Barely a year after the purchase, we began to experience moisture at almost every part of the Church hall, staining the Church curtains and everything we put on the wall, oh, it was very ugly. At first, we thought we can just fix it easily through scraping and painting of the wall, but all to no avail, we invited the building engineers from the local authorities and we are told that the problem comes from water leakage coming from the general water pipeline, and we would not have been affected if the foundation has been well fortified with the necessary materials to resist water leakage, or, had a flood of any magnitude, according to the basic general construction standard given to every builder.

Because of negligence on the part of the builder, this whole new building will begin to experience the effect of damp in every area unless the necessary measures were implemented in fixing the foundation, which of course is more costlier than laying it right in the first place.

Thank God a lasting solution has been found to get rid of the damp, it is somehow well covered for now and the water company has come to fix the broken pipe, unfortunately, the wall is still wet inside, though the wall is covered, but the foundation is still left unrepaired.

We had made a permanent decision based on insufficient information. We can give any excuse to justify ourselves; you might as well say the same thing about; 'how do I know the person I am getting married to'? Or, 'Where does he come from?' Or, how does that matter to me?

How do I know that business is going to fail or succeed? But the fact of the matter is, that we were not foundation conscious at the time the purchase was made, we are more building conscious than foundation conscious. We can say of course, 'how do you expect me to know what the foundation is made of?' Or 'do you expect me to dig the foundation to be able to know the type of materials the foundation is made of?

Had we been foundation minded before we made the purchase, we would have asked for the building plans and history from the builders, or checked with the town council authority, to know every detail of the building, but we bought the building and neglected the most important part.

I learnt a great and bitter lesson about the importance of foundations through this experience, how about you? Are you foundation conscious?

You might also want to say 'how does that concern me'? Don't forget, that whosoever buys the building also purchases what it was built on.

It is our responsibility to get all possible information about the person you are going to be spending the rest of your life with, the business you are going to spend all your hard earned money on, the career that is going to shape your entire life, or, the ministry you will be giving account of at the end of your life's journey, it is your responsibility to find out and know whether he or she has suffered any kind of abuse during their childhood, you are supposed to know if he or she had any previous relationships and what led to their failure, It is your responsibility to know if he or she is the one that loves the Lord or is one who only opens his Bible or goes to church when asked to, if he or she has ever been sacked from work or suspended from college. If the answer is yes, you have a right to know why?

What kinds of friends is he or she keeping, study and consider what he spends his money on, how about his or her financial management? Etc. The same thing applies to your business and every other commitment that could affect your life and the lives of the people in your life. When you do all these as you are entering into a serious relationship or about to make a serious decision, you will be a wise builder, building on a solid foundation for the future.

Does that picture your life, your marriage, your career, your business etc.? Have you made a life changing decision based on little or no information? Are your decisions based on the appearance rather than the reality? Have you entered into marriage without the foundation in mind? Are you regretting right now of ever getting married to your spouse? Are you becoming conscious of the wrong foundation you have laid in your business and you feel you should not have put your money on it in the first place? Is there any remedy to your broken foundations?

If the foundations are destroyed, what can the righteous do?

What kind of foundations is the Lord talking about?

To start with, the Bible says *"If the foundations are destroyed* "foundations here is plural and not singular, we have only one foundation of faith, which is Jesus Christ and no other foundation can be laid other than that which is laid which is Jesus Christ (1 Corinthians 3:11) and besides, this foundation is indestructible for the Scripture said *"Behold, I lay in Zion for a foundation a stone, a tried stone, a precious stone, a sure foundation;"* (Isa. 28:16)

In Psalm 11:1, David was advised to "Run to the mountain (MSG)." David is saying, "How can you ask me to run away? I have put my trust in the Lord." But these people who are his advisers reminded him that there are people who are after his life. Furthermore, this is a time when the foundations have been destroyed, and the question is asked, "If the foundations be destroyed, what can the righteous do." The foundations that are spoken of in this verse are the foundations of equity, justice, morality and order that support a society—those foundations that keep a culture from falling.

In your own case, it could be the foundation of your marriage, or foundation of your Ministry, or foundation of your business or career. But David is living in a time when these foundations have been destroyed. David lives in a period of time when that particular society was in a state of total confusion and disorder. The nation and the community are totally corrupt. If it is true that David is living in such a time of lawlessness and complete ungodliness, what can righteous people do when they find themselves living in a period of such disorder and confusion? What can the righteous accomplish when the whole society has been pulled apart?

This is a relevant question for us in these days, because, as Christians, we are facing precisely the same situation that David faced in Psalm 11. We live in the world where the foundations are being destroyed. We are witnessing a violent attack to remove the foundations on which our faith was founded.

Our founding fathers of faith based their ideas of a godly standard of living on equality among the races, freedom from oppression and justice for the poor, the sick and weak in society. Those foundations are being destroyed, for in this age of religious tolerance and pluralism our world has been invaded by groups of intolerant religious fanatics who are bent on harassing, intimidating, disrupting, murdering and violating our precious freedoms, those foundations have been destroyed, when we are told that no one religion should influence the decisions of those in political power.

As a matter of fact, we are told that those in authority should not be influenced by any kind of religious beliefs when they are making political decisions today

Our precious foundations for society had been that of morality based upon the Word of God, but since we have rejected the Word of God as the foundation of morality, one person's concept of what is right and wrong is as good as the next person's. When such a situation exists, eventually there will be no basis for determining what is right or wrong other than what is decided upon by a majority, or by those who have the most political or military power.

One of the foundations we held high was that of protecting and supporting the ideal of biblical family life, but our families are being destroyed because the Biblical concepts of father, mother, husband, wife, marriage, and children are no longer followed.

We no longer build our families on the solid rock of God's Word, but on the ever-shifting, ever-changing sands of public opinion. The fundamental Biblical concept of marriage as established by God himself which stipulate marriage to be a matrimony between a man and a woman has been destroyed by the ambitious and godless politicians of our time, who, because of their political ambitions are ready to compromise even their faith by recognizing and legalizing same sex marriage and thereby destroying our fundamental family values.

Those foundations have been destroyed, when the governments are coming up with their so called child protection laws, allowing a child as young as sixteen years of age to have an abortion without parental knowledge and consent.

Those foundations have been destroyed by some gullible religious leaders, who adulterated the precious 'Gospel of the Kingdom' to fit in to their way of life, who choose to be 'a man of the people' instead of a 'man of God'. How do we live in a society when these foundations have been destroyed? Do we run as cowards to the mountain as David is advised to do in the book of Psalm and run in fear because the ungodly are in power, or is there some other response that is more appropriate for the people of God?

Day by day, more and more foundations are being shaken in our world, our lives, our marriages and in our society. Economic and political changes appear to be on the horizon that will threaten our entire way of life. What can we do if the economic foundations of our countries are destroyed?

As we look at how laws and the Constitutions are being reinterpreted to mean things totally different from what was really intended, we see that the foundations of our government itself are being destroyed. What can the righteous, the believers in Jesus Christ do, when the foundations of a society are destroyed?

Christians are the only people that are being addressed and who are expected to answer these all-important questions.

When the foundations are destroyed, it will become very difficult for many people. They can feel as if the world has come to an end. They can become hopeless and depressed.

However, there is an answer to this question, "What can the righteous do?" This question does not end in hopeless surrender, but in a bold reaffirmation of faith.

To begin with, people might have always been able to say with Job, "The Lord gives, and the Lord takes away, blessed be the name of the Lord." Whatever we might not have that we used to have, God has deemed fit at this particular time to allow us to be deprived of it.

God has divine reasons for even allowing the foundations to be destroyed. But even if the foundations are destroyed, look at what David says in verse 4: "*The Lord is in his holy temple, the Lord's throne is in heaven.*" Even if the foundations of our society are destroyed God's foundations remain firm. Paul wrote, "*Nevertheless, the foundation of God standeth sure, having this seal, The Lord knoweth them that are his . . .*"

(2 Timothy 2:19),

The foundations of His government can never be destroyed. If all the banks fail, if our business crumbles and our life savings and our life's work is snatched away from us, the Christian can still go through it all because his treasure is not on earth. His treasure is in heaven where moth and rust cannot corrupt, where thieves cannot break in and steal. As a result of this, while the Christian can experience hurt at the loss of many things, he looks up to heaven and sees his treasure there, eternally safe and secure, and that holy assurances calms his mind and his fears.

So many times we behave exactly like the people of the world, don't we? We experience loss and we say, "I am ruined, I am finished!" But the Christian can never be ruined. His work was finished on the cross so that it will not be finished for you or me. The people of this world lose this world's goods and say, "I have lost everything." The Christian can never make that statement.

The Christian can never say, "I have lost everything," because if you are a Christian, Christ becomes your everything, and there is no way that you can lose Him unless you choose to leave Him. He is always there to receive you, He said;" And call upon me in the day of trouble: I will deliver thee, and thou shalt glorify me." (Psalm 50:15) Christ, Who is 'Your Everything' is seated on His throne, the throne that has a foundation that can never be shaken.

What can the righteous do? The righteous can put their faith (trust) in the 'Lord of lords' and the 'King of kings', the 'Captain of our salvation', the sovereign Lord of heaven and earth, even when foundations of our society are crumbling; His is bound to stand for eternity. Remember the word of the Lord to King Solomon in 2 Chronicles 7:12-16.

"Then the Lord appeared to Solomon by night, and said to him: "I have heard your prayer, and have chosen this place for Myself as a house of sacrifice. 13 When I shut up heaven and there is no rain, or command the locusts to devour the land, or send pestilence among My people, 14 if My people who are called by My name will humble themselves, and pray and seek My face, and turn from their wicked ways, then I will hear from heaven, and will forgive their sin and heal their land. 15 Now My eyes will be open and My ears attentive to prayer made in this place. 16 For now I have chosen and sanctified this house, that My name may be there forever; and My eyes and My heart will be there perpetually".

If the foundations are destroyed, **what can the righteous do?** The righteous can happily look beyond the present circumstances to the promising future. If there is somebody out there who is supposed to be able to see something good, even in the darkest moments, these are the Believers in Jesus Christ believing in the fact that He is coming back. I know that we get irritated with those people who can always look on the bright side, people who can see the silver lining in every cloud, but the Christian certainly ought to be able to find something to be thankful for even in the midst of the most terrible circumstances. We know that all things work together for good, for those who love God, for those who are the called according to his purpose.

(Romans 8:28)

The destruction of the foundations of our society is not a good thing, but God can cause even that destruction to eventually work together for our good.

Maybe upon the fall of this society, God is going to erect something even better, something nobler, and something that will last and stand the test of time. Even when the foundations are being destroyed, we can see, as the writer to the Hebrews put it;

"The removing of those things that are shaken, as of things that are made, that those things which cannot be shaken may remain"

(Heb. 12:27).

If the foundations are destroyed, **what can the righteous do?** We can look forward to that city whose builder and maker is God (Heb. 11:10). The righteous can also look forward to receiving that kingdom which cannot be moved.

(Heb. 12:28).

If the foundations are destroyed, **what can the righteous do?** The righteous can carry on living by Christ's teaching in Matthew chapters 5, 6 and 7. Just because the world is crumbling and the social order is deteriorating, that does not free us of our responsibility to obey Jesus and rebuild the foundations. It is tempting in these days to run to the mountains, to give up on the world and everyone in it. Nevertheless, we must continue to proclaim the kingdom of God is at hand, even in a world that is hostile to it. "For we can do nothing against the truth, but for the truth."

(2 Cor. 13:8).

If the foundations are destroyed, **what can the righteous do?** We must live in such a way as to show others how right it is to live according to God's word as the Scripture says "Let your light so shine before men, that they may see your good works, and glorify your Father which is in heaven (Matthew 5:16). We must take our stand through prayer, intercession, and the way we live, we must continue to share the words of God, we must walk the walk of Jesus and take our stand against the wiles of the devil. If we don't stand for something, we will fall for anything, we must stand for Jesus Christ in the midst of pressing needs and challenges as the Scripture says *"yea, let God be true, but every man a liar, as it is written, That thou mightest be justified in thy sayings, and mightest overcome when thou art judged."* (Rom. 3:4)

Even if the judicial system becomes corrupt, and the people in authority pervert justice, we have a responsibility to live according to the laws Jesus taught us to live by, to uphold His teaching. The world will follow the devil, but we still have the responsibility to keep ourselves unspotted from the world. Christians have often found themselves in those places where the foundations had been removed, but they did not withdraw and give up. They continued to struggle, to fight, and to overcome in the name of Jesus Christ.

It is easy to be obedient and upright when the whole society is supportive. The actual test of our faith comes, when we found ourselves in a world where the foundations have been destroyed.

In such moments we may be tempted to give up the struggle, to give up to the corruptions and immoralities of this world, to give up on spreading the good news of the kingdom of God.

If the foundations are been destroyed, **what can the righteous do?** They can do what the disciples of the upper room did some 2,000 years ago after they had been baptized in the Holy Spirit. They can turn the world upside down through their fervent prayers and intercessions.

If the foundations are destroyed, **what can the righteous do?** The righteous can relay a new and better foundation by preaching the gospel of the kingdom, with signs and wonders following, taking Christ to their community and their neighbours, when someone is led to Christ, a new foundation of Christ is being laid, in the life and family of that person.

After all, these other things that we look upon as the foundation of our lives and our society are actually not real firm foundations at all. The law, economics, justice, concepts of freedom, not even the Constitution of our countries, can be firm foundations. The only firm, lasting, foundation is our Lord Jesus Christ Himself.

Jesus said, "*Therefore whosoever heareth these sayings of mine, and doeth them, I will liken him unto a wise man, which built his house upon a rock, and the rain descended, and the floods came, and the winds blew, and beat upon that house; and it fell not: for it was founded upon a rock.*

And every one that heareth these sayings of mine, and doeth them not, shall be likened unto a foolish man, which built his house upon the sand: And the rain descended, and the floods came, and the winds blew, and beat upon that house; and it fell: and great was the fall of it"

(Matt. 7:24-27).

Any nation, any family, any person that does not build on the foundation of Christ's teachings and ends up living in disobedience to His words is doomed to ultimately face rejection from the very one they seek to be accepted by. That nation, that family, that person, that ministry, that business may stand for a long time, but when the times of great testing come, will they finish by being able to stand before Him?

What can the righteous do? The righteous can build their lives on Christ's doctrines, His teachings and that simply means, doing what He askes His disciple's to do, that can be found easily by reading the New Testament.

Get a bible, learn His words, note who He is speaking to, take note of His words, when He says to His disciples to forgive, He is talking to you and me, for we are also His disciples.

He also makes short cuts to make it easier, He says, treat others in the same way you want them to treat you, WOW, that is so simple, but so powerful. He closes in the last chapter of Revelation by pointing out that what you do is very important.

Remember, Christianity is not Christianity if all you use is your ears, if you believe the ship may sink but still board the ship and set sail for the destination, I would say you really did not believe it would sink, when it does sink and you drown, whose fault was that?

Are you walking as He walked? Are you living as He lived? In closing let me ask; what is the state of your foundation? Is there forgiveness for a Christian who has lived a disobedient and rebellious life?

In Revelation chapter 2 and 3, Some are told that what they are doing is unacceptable, and if they (these Christians) don't repent they are in for serious consequences, they are, apart from some in Thyatira who had been given the chance but had refused to repent, the others were being given the opportunity to repent, to change their minds, their thoughts, the way they thought and this would begin to change what they were doing, to stop what is not what Jesus taught and start doing what Jesus taught, that is true repentance, living as Jesus said his followers are to live.

If you don't live your life in harmony with the doctrine of Christ, you don't love Him! Now that is strong words, but, if I love you, or at the least care for you, I will dare to stick my neck out and tell you the real truth!

Jesus and His finished work on the Cross purchased our forgiveness, He is the reason we are forgiven and Him alone, we are given the power to become the children of The Father, however, His teaching on how we are to live is our opportunity to demonstrate we have repented and we do believe His word and we really do love Him.

Our obedience to Christ's teachings are the ultimate foundation upon which we are to build our Christian life, and doing so we are keeping our wonderful garments clean and undefiled, we, the righteous, can keep on trusting God as we live a life following, seeking, asking and obeying Jesus, **the righteous** can labour and fight with all their might hoping to see people and nations of the world receive Christ as Lord and Saviour, yet have full assurance that we are guaranteed full and absolute salvation in Christ.

His word has become our solid foundation, how? By never losing sight of who He makes us when we abide in Him and His Word abides in us, we are in Him when we live a life following Him, He is where our true destiny leads, this is for everyone who loves Him and proves it by obeying His Words.

Remember, if you don't read His Words, how can you know His Words? How can you claim His promises? If you don't know what He said, how can you do what He said? It is simple, 'You can't'!

If the foundations are destroyed, **what can the righteous do?** The righteous should constantly, repeatedly, meditatively and prayerfully study the word of God, for *the Word of God is living and powerful . . ." (Hebrew 4:12)* In His word there is power, directions, guidance, protections, healings, solutions, provisions, fulfilments and hope etc. *"How can a young man cleanse his way? By taking heed according to Your word With my whole heart have I sought thee: O let me not wander from thy commandments. Thy word have I hid in mine heart, that I might not sin against thee"*

(Psalm 119:9-11).

The word of God will keep you from sin otherwise sin could keep you away from the word of God. Discover what He said; then, begin to do what He required of those who choose to follow Him. Only by so doing will you become a true disciple of Jesus Christ today!

My friend, no matter how bad the state of your physical foundations, no matter the hopelessness of its conditions, it's not too late to restore it back again, just take a visit to the to the potter's house, He will put it right again *"The word which came to Jeremiah from the LORD, saying: ² "Arise and go down to the potter's house, and there I will cause you to hear My words."*

³ Then I went down to the potter's house, and there he was, making something at the wheel. ⁴ And the vessel that he made of clay was marred in the hand of the potter; so he made it again into another vessel, as it seemed good to the potter to make.

(Jeremiah 18:1-4)

The restoration of your foundations is in the hand of the most high God, for He is the Foundation of the foundations, talk to Jesus who is the foundation of your faith today with the readiness to change, learn your lessons, amend your ways, study His word and pray the prayer, *"Commit thy works unto the LORD, and thy thoughts shall be established*

(Proverbs 16:3)

It's not too late to change, if you are reading this and now realize you have been building your life on sand, turn to Jesus and ask Him to forgive you, repent, and then actively start building your life on the foundation that Jesus defines in His teachings, read Matthew Chapters 5, 6 and 7 and start to live a life in real obedience and experience a life of fulfilment with God's love in it, with a real expectant hope and life changing faith.

About The Author

REVEREND NELSON OLANREWAJU Olajide is the Founder and senior pastor of the Living Spring Ministry with the headquarters on the island of Tenerife, part of Spanish territory, and having branches across Europe. In 1982, he was converted and became a Christian, having formerly been in the Islamic religion and since then has never looked back. His passion for souls and dedication to the 'Good News of the Kingdom of Heaven', along with his commitment to preaching and spread the Good News of Jesus Christ both to the lost and saved, have taken him far and wide. In 1992 he visited the Caribbean island of Jamaica where he worked as a full time missionary with an International ministry, later moving to Panama. In 1998, God led him to open the Living Spring Pentecostal Church in Spain and since then the Church has grown numerically and spiritually, with many souls getting saved with diverse signs and wonders following. He has also obtained a degree in Theology and Biblical Counseling. Rev. Olajide is a dynamic teacher and Bible expositor, anointed Preacher and a gifted Family Counselor. His calling has taken him across the continent of Africa, Spain, UK, Germany, Norway, USA etc. He is married to Mary Olajide and blessed with two children. He lives presently in Spain with his family.